Bristol F2B Fighter

King of Two-Seaters

Above:
Start-up. A No 11 Squadron warming up for a sortie. Note that the wheel fabric covers have been removed here, revealing wire 'spokes'; bomb racks are visible under each lower wing and fuselage. *Via K. M. Molson*

Below:
An Arab-engined F2B of No 8 Squadron at Malincourt on 11 November 1918. Note the bomb racks under the wings.
Via G. Stuart Leslie

Bristol F2B Fighter

King of Two-Seaters

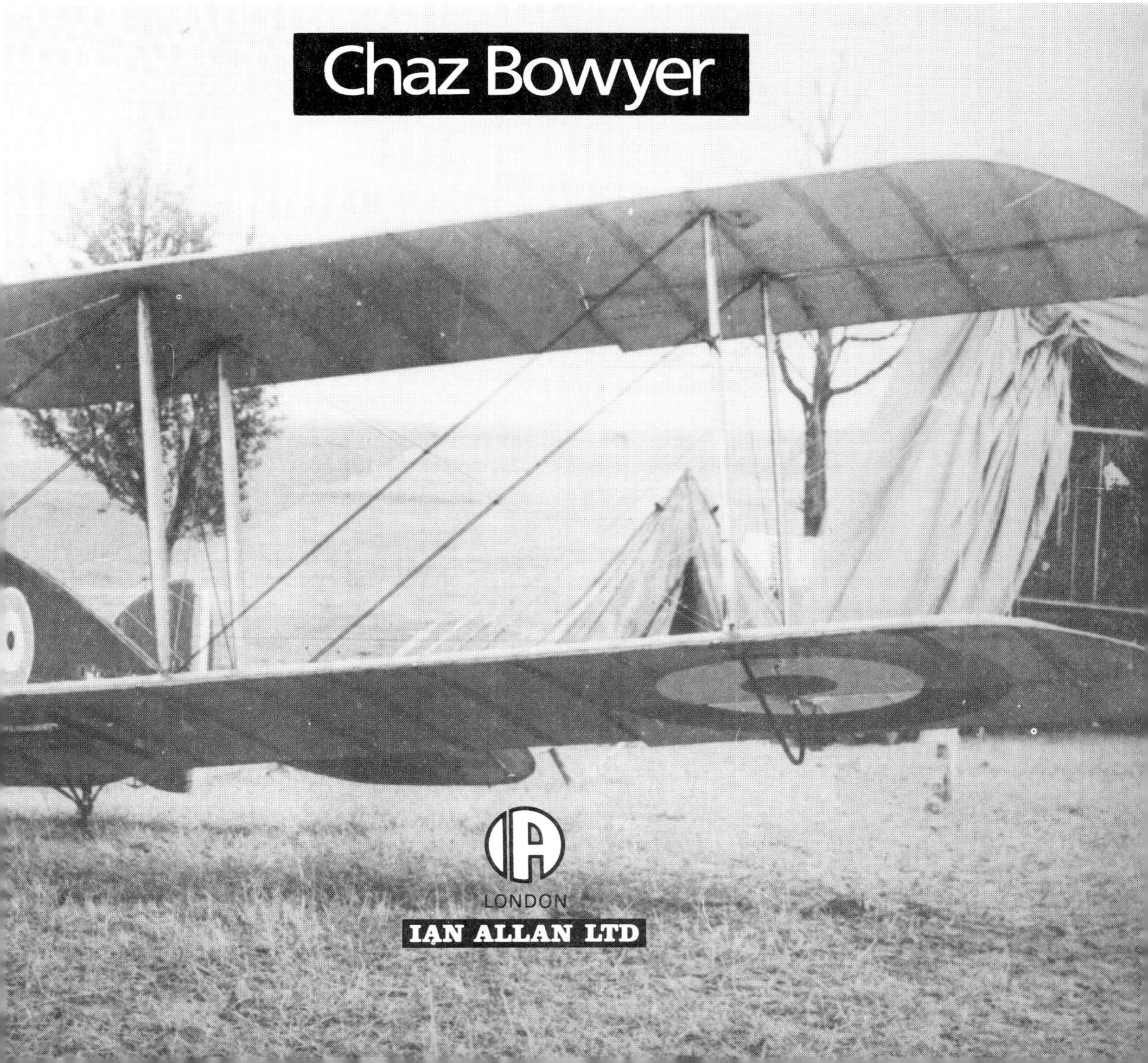

Chaz Bowyer

LONDON

IAN ALLAN LTD

By the same author
Calshot, 1913-61
The Flying Elephants — 27 Squadron RFC/RAF
Mosquito at War
Hurricane at War
Airmen of World War One
Sunderland at War
Hampden Special
Beaufighter at War
Path Finders at War
Albert Ball, VC
For Valour — The Air VCs
Sopwith Camel — King of Combat
History of the RAF
Guns in the Sky — The AGs
Coastal Command at War
Spitfire
Fighter Command, 1936-68
Surviving Aircraft of World War Two
Age of the Biplane
Air War over Europe, 1939-45
Desert Air Force at War (*co-author*)
Encyclopaedia of British Military Aircraft
Bomber Group at War
Wellington at War
Images of Air War, 1939-45
Bomber Barons
Eugene Esmonde, VC, DSO
Royal Air Force Handbook, 1939-45
Bristol Blenheim
Fighter Pilots of the RAF, 1939-45
Mosquito Squadrons of the RAF
Men of the Desert Air Force, 1940-43
Gloster Meteor
Men of Coastal Command, 1939-45

Edited
Bomber Pilot, 1916-18
Fighter Pilot on the Western Front
Wings over the Somme
Fall of an Eagle — Ernst Udet

First published 1985

ISBN 0 7110 1562 7

Published by Ian Allan Ltd, Shepperton, Surrey; and printed by Ian Allan Printing Ltd at their works at Coombelands in Runnymede, England

Contents

Preface

By early 1916 the burgeoning aerial war above the Western Front in France had already established a crucial need of all participating air services for aircraft which would not simply perform their prime role of reconnaissance but would also be capable of a pure combat role. The Bristol F2B Fighter skilfully 'married' both of those roles and during 1917-18 became acknowledged as the finest example of its type to fly operationally, truly earning its unofficial title of 'King of the Two-Seaters'. Had those years been the F2B's sole contribution to aviation history it would have fully justified a permanent niche in the annals of aerial warfare, yet it was destined to continue in first-line service with the RAF until 1932. During those post-bellum years Bristol F2Bs and their indefatigable crews flew virtual unceasing warlike operations in foreign skies, despite increasing obsolescence and deteriorating maintenance facilities, and little altered from its original design.

Within the necessary limitations of any single volume, I have attempted in this book to present the development and, especially, the operational career of the Bristol Fighter, albeit in somewhat condensed form. Although certain technical details are included here, readers seeking greater technical data in depth are commended to the already published works by J. M. Bruce and C. H. Barnes et al, listed in my select bibliography. For enormous and unselfish assistance in my own research, and particularly in the context of photographic and other illustrations herein, I would like to record my deep gratitude to the following friends and fellow aviation 'Knuts', listed in no significant order of importance: C. H. Barnes; J. M. Bruce; A. E. Ferko; Flt Lt A. Thomas, RAF; G. Stuart Leslie; P. G. Cooksley; C. Huston; J. H. Hume; N. L. R. Franks; C. C. H. Cole; R. W. Mack of the RAF Museum; C. A. Owers; R. Vann; D. Gray of Walkers Studios, Scarborough; Lt-Col Avi M. Terlinden; J. B. Cynk; Z. Hurt.

I would also thank Mr Rupert Harvey for permission to quote certain extracts from the published works of his late father, Maj W. J. F. Harvey MBE, DFC, TD; and the late Air Cdre A. H. Wheeler CBE, MA, FRAeS, for similar consent to reproduce an extract from his book *Flying Between the Wars* (G. T. Foulis, 1972).

Chaz Bowyer
Norwich
1985

Left:
F2Bs of No 14 Squadron (nearest, J6648) at the opening of Jerusalem's aerodrome in May 1924.
G. Stuart Leslie

Below:
Capt Frank Sowter Barnwell OBE, AFC, BSc, chief designer of the Bristol F2B Fighter.
British Aerospace

Genesis

On 19 February 1910 the Bristol-born millionaire pioneer of electric tramways, Sir George White Bt, formed four companies simultaneously, each for the purpose of developing some facet of commercial aircraft. While three of these companies were registered with purely nominal capital (merely £100 apiece), the fourth, named The British & Colonial Aeroplane Co Ltd, became his premier trading company, and by August 1911 Filton House, some four miles from Bristol City centre, had been acquired as the company's general offices, next to two iron sheds leased from the Bristol Tramways Co which comprised the initial factory. As Sir George assembled his staff of administrators and technical personnel, these included Frank Sowter Barnwell, who joined the firm in March 1911 as a draughtsman and was destined to become the firm's chief engineer and a major influence on Bristol aircraft designs for the next 27 years.

Born in Lewisham, Kent in 1880, Frank Barnwell was educated at Fettes in Scotland after his family had moved to Glasgow, and from 1898 to 1904 served an apprenticeship with the Fairfield Shipbuilding Co at Govan — in which his father was a partner — and spent his spare time studying at the Technical College and Glasgow University, obtaining a BSc degree in naval architecture in 1905. From then until joining the Bristol firm, Barnwell had spent a year in America with a shipbuilding firm, then returned to Britain to join two of his brothers in their own small engineering firm, constructing gliders and powered aeroplanes. In 1912 Barnwell became a member of the Royal Aero Club, and in 1913 was responsible for the design and stressing calculations for a new aircraft, the now-famous Bristol Scout single-seat biplane which, with the famed Australian Harry Busteed at its controls, reached a speed of 97mph in February 1914 and was recognised as an outstanding design among its contemporaries. With the outbreak of war in the autumn of 1914 the War Office policy of restricting all aeroplane design to the Royal Aircraft Factory, Farnborough saw the Bristol Co's Filton factory wholly engaged in contracted production of the Farnborough-designed BE2c aircraft for the RFC and RNAS, apart from a handful of orders for Bristol Scouts; a situation which left Barnwell and his colleagues virtually nothing creative to do. The result was that Frank Barnwell left the firm to join the RFC, obtaining his RAeC pilot certificate, No 986, on 9 December 1914, and being awarded his RFC wings at Upavon in March 1915, at the age of 35. He was then posted to No 12 Squadron RFC to fly Avro 504s and BE2cs at Netheravon under the command of Maj Cyril Newall (later, MRAF Baron Newall, Chief of Air Staff 1937-40), being promoted to Captain.

In the interim an outcry in Parliament against the tragic losses among RFC airmen in France, particularly the crews of the Royal Aircraft Factory's BE2cs, led to pressure for the War Office to give wider recognition to the aircraft designs of private firms — something already acknowledged by the Admiralty for its own air service — and one outcome was that Capt Barnwell RFC was given 'indefinite leave' (without Service pay . . .) in order to rejoin the Bristol Co in August 1915 as its chief designer. Barnwell, on taking up his new appointment, selected as his principal assistant a youthful graduate of Bristol University, L. G. Frise, who, like Barnwell, had been 'released' from his commission in the RNAS. Barnwell's immediate tasks on returning to his civilian desk were to design two new aircraft, a single-seat fighter and a two-seat reconnaissance machine. The former emerged as the M.1 monoplane in July 1916, while the latter was intended as a replacement for the much-vilified BE2c. Based broadly on the RFC HQ specifications issued in late 1915 for a corps reconnaissance and artillery-spotting two-seater capable of defending itself — a clear acknowledgement of the BE2c's extreme vulnerability in aerial combat — Barnwell drew up the design of a two-bay, equal-span biplane in March 1916 titled R2A.

Originally designed to have a 120hp Beardmore

Above:

The first Bristol F2A, A3303, in its original form with wing root endplates, vertical flank radiators, lack of rear cockpit coaming, gap between lower wings and BE-type wings (modified). It is seen here at Filton in September 1916. *Bristol Aeroplane Co*

Right:

A3303 about to be air-tested at Filton in September 1916. *Via C. H. Barnes*

engine, the R2A placed the pilot in the front seat with his Observer/Gunner immediately behind him, back to back, for close crew co-operation. Bearing in mind the BE2c's cramped crew locations, virtually surrounded by a birdcage of struts and wires, Barnwell had the R2A's fuselage placed midway between the wings, with the upper mainplane at pilot's eye-level, thereby giving him an excellent field of vision upwards, downwards and forward; while the rear gunner's field of fire was enhanced by having the fuselage designed to taper markedly in depth towards the tailplane, and placing more than a third of the fin and rudder empennage below tailplane level. This, combined with the location of the upper wing, gave an R2A gunner the ability to fire in a 360deg circle over the aircraft and a wide field downwards in most directions. Armament in the R2A consisted of a fixed Lewis gun forward for the pilot, and a 'free' Lewis gun on an Etévé rotating mounting for the gunner. The rear cockpit was quite well furnished for its occupant, having a folding seat, wireless, camera, message-launching tube and dual controls in case the pilot became incapacitated. While the R2A design ostensibly fulfilled the official requirements, Barnwell considered it under-powered, and in May 1916, in the hope of obtaining a 150hp Hispano Suiza engine, he produced a redesign around such a power plant, which he titled R2B. Though essentially similar in most respects to its predecessor, the R2B was an unequal span biplane with strut-braced wing extensions and slightly shorter length of fuselage.

In July 1916, however, Barnwell was able to obtain not only a 150hp Hispano Suiza but also a new 190hp Rolls-Royce engine, and immediately set to work to redesign his R2B project for installation of both power installations. In the case of the Rolls-Royce engine he also took the opportunity to refine the general layout of the aircraft, its fuselage, armament and other details. Reverting first to equal-span wings, Barnwell retained the mid-gap location of the fuselage, but further refined the rear fuselage by extending the downward curve of its upper longerons towards a horizontal knife-edge terminal on the rear spar of the (now) adjustable tailplane, thus improving the rear gunner's fire-arc. The introduction of an adjustable tailplane meant that incidence could be varied to give stable 'hands-off' flying at most speeds. The gunner's cockpit was revised internally, replacing the former fold-up seat with a slide-mounted fore-and-aft arrangement, while the dual controls were replaced by a small emergency lever and socket for restricted elevator control and hand-grips on the rudder cables. New fuel and oil tank installations proved necessary, and Barnwell also improved the forward armament by installing a standard Vickers 0.303in machine gun along the centre-line in a tunnel through the upper fuel tank. By this arrangement the gun's cocking handle sat immediately in front of the pilot, and the gun benefited from the warm air from the engine in preventing freezing of its mechanism and feed. The resulting design was titled F2A — the 'F' to indicate Barnwell's conception of the aircraft as a fighter rather than simply a reconnaissance machine — and work began on constructing two prototype F2As in July 1916: one (A3303) to have the Rolls-Royce engine, and the other (A3304) the Hispano Suiza. Production of both prototypes and a further 50 production machines (A3305-A3354) was officially sanctioned by Contract No 87/A/552 dated 28 August 1916.

The first prototype F2A, A3303, appeared at the beginning of September 1916. In its original form the engine installation had two vertical flank radiators either side of the rear nose cowling which tended to obscure the pilot's forward vision, while the lower wings had a gap centrally. The fuselage, though conforming with Barnwell's design in general, had no top decking on its rear section and had no form of gun mounting for the rear cockpit; the lower wing roots had end-plates mounted. In this form A3303 made its first air test flight on 9 September 1916 and then went to CFS, Upavon for official acceptance flight trials on 21 September. These trials resulted in several recommendations for further modifications, particularly the removal of the somewhat ugly vertical radiators

Top:
A3304, the second prototype F2A, at Filton in December 1916, with gun ring added, lower wings 'gap' filled and forward longerons modified to F2B standard, and new circular radiator. *Bristol Aeroplane Co*

Above:
Production F2A, A3314, prior to a factory air test. *A. Tidmarsh*

and their replacement by a single frontal nose radiator. Returning to Upavon in mid-October, the slightly modified A3303 was given a generally favourable report. By then the second prototype, A3304, was ready for testing with its Hispano engine already fitted with a circular nose radiator although otherwise closely resembling its stablemate F2A. Both machines at that stage employed adapted BE2-type wings with modified trailing edges, and both had end-plates fitted to the roots of their lower wings. In view of the non-availability of further Hispano engines, it was decided to fit the 190hp Rolls-Royce engine (later titled Falcon I) in production F2As, and first deliveries of these commenced on 20 December 1916 from Bristol's Brislington factory.

In the interim the second prototype, A3304, had undergone its official trials at Upavon on 4 and 6 December, but in further modified form resulting from the recommendations of the CFS pilots after testing A3303. These modifications now included filling the gap in the lower wings and removing the wing root end-plates, and sloping the upper longerons forward of the pilot's cockpit downwards to improve forward vision. This latter improvement gave a taper to the forward fuselage top decking and permitted fitment of a larger upper tank and ammunition box for the pilot's Vickers machine gun. In this modified form the machine was redesignated as F2B, approved for full production, and a further contract for 200 machines of F2B standard was issued. As production of F2Bs got under way more powerful Rolls-Royce engines became available — the Falcon II of 220hp and, later, the Falcon III of 275hp — and were fitted into production F2Bs as and when supply of either was practicable over the following year. One other modification incorporated in production F2Bs gave the aircraft raked wing-tips in place of the BE-type outlines of the two prototypes. By late March 1917 the 50th production aircraft had left Bristol's factory, while on 13 April deliveries of the initial 200-batch of F2Bs commenced.

In the same month, July 1916, that Frank Barnwell had drafted the revision of the R2A design to accept a 190hp Rolls-Royce engine, he also produced preliminary drawings for a parallel project, the MR1 all-metal biplane. The possibilities for all-metal constructed aircraft had been investigated by the Bristol firm for several years,

Below:
Production F2A, A3329, at Beaulieu on 19 July 1917. *E. J. Watkins*

and the MR1 exemplified Barnwell's personal convictions of the efficacy of metal-skeleton aircraft, and although the detail design of the MR1 was then given to Wilfrid T. Reid to complete, the outcome machine bore more than a passing resemblance to Barnwell's R2A/F2A designs. A contract for just two prototype MR1s was awarded on 2 November 1916, and the first of these, A5177, was completed (except for its wings) by mid-1917. Fitted temporarily with conventional wood-structure wings for air evaluation, A5177 passed its tests and was handed over to the Air Board on 23 December 1917. This machine then underwent a series of structural tests and trials, providing much information for future ideas on metal-framed aircraft, being renumbered as A58623 at a later stage. The second MR1 prototype, A5178, was eventually flown with metal wings in late 1918, powered by a 170hp Wolseley Viper engine, and was occasionally flown by Barnwell. Accepted by the RAE, Farnborough for further evaluation, MR1 A5178 was flown to Farnborough on 19 April 1919 by Barnwell, but in landing he collided with a tree near the north gate of the RAE, and crashed, without serious injury to himself but damaging the MR1 sufficiently to deter the RAE from attempting to repair the machine.

By early 1917, apart from a number of individual Bristol F2As already serving on various RFC experimental and training units, the first all-F2A unit, No 48 Squadron RFC at Rendcombe, began replacing its obsolete BE12 so-termed 'fighters' with the new F2As in February 1917 and began working up on these in preparation for an imminent move to France for operations over the Western Front. Finally, commanded by Maj A. V. 'Zulu' Bettington and comprising 16 officers and 83 other ranks, No 48 Squadron arrived at Bellevue aerodrome in France on 8 March 1917, sharing this airfield and its accommodation with No 6 Squadron RNAS (Nieuport Scouts) and No 59 Squadron RFC (RE8s). Here 48's aircrews continued their operational pre-training though as yet they were forbidden to fly over enemy territory, being deliberately kept in abeyance to await the start of an Allied land offensive — the First Battle of the Scarpe, or more familiarly, the Battle of Arras — due in early April 1917. With few exceptions, the squadron's aircrews were about to experience aerial combat for the first time. Eager as these were to 'join the war', it would seem to be yet another overt example of confused reasoning by the RFC hierarchy in 'Bolo House' to give a new air weapon to untried men. Nevertheless, to No 48 Squadron fell the privilege of introducing the Bristol Fighter — the name already permanently associated with Frank Barnwell's brainchild — to its true vocation.

Above:
The first Bristol MR1, A5177, an all-metal constructed machine. Of its four main bolted fuselage sections, the section containing the rear cockpit could (theoretically) be removed to convert the aircraft to a single-seat fighter.
Bristol Aeroplane Co

Into Combat

As the crews of No 48 Squadron prepared for their operational debut with their Bristol F2As, emphasis was laid upon tight formation-keeping as a general defensive tactic, enabling all Observer-gunners to interlace their fire arcs and thereby put up — hopefully — a strong deterrent 'barrage' against any enemy fighter opposition. The pure *fighting* potential of the F2A design had yet to be perceived fully; understandably so since it was, ostensibly, simply a replacement for the outmoded BE2c in *reconnaissance* roles. Thus the F2A's armament, though a patent improvement over the makeshift arrangements of the BE, was initially regarded more as a *defensive* protection rather than offensive weaponry while the crews carried out their prime function of gathering intelligence for their army commanders. Such a concept inevitably engendered a defensive stance when first the F2A crews clashed with German fighters with the Bristols' pilots automatically adopting the contemporary two-seater tactics of manoeuvring to enable their gunners to deal with any opposition. While such tactics had been the only possible salvation for the vulnerable BEs, they were in a sense self-defeating in the case of the Bristol Fighter which, unlike the highly stable BE, possessed a single-seat fighter's combat manoeuvrability, good structural strength, and a fighter-like performance; assets which meant it could take on any existing enemy fighters on at least near-equal terms if handled to its full capabilities. Moreover, it had the 'bonus' of a rear gun defence/offence when required, something unavailable to any single-seat fighter.

While the foregoing comment, albeit made with the golden advantage of hindsight many decades after the events, remains valid, its essence has, unfortunately, become the basis for a near-myth perpetuated by many historians and other authors since 1918 virtually condemning the tactics and fighting record of No 48 Squadron's first Bristol F2A crews during April-June 1917, by quoting actions out of full context and over-emphasising the squadron's losses without also pointing to the crews' successes. A closer scrutiny of those initial weeks of F2A operations produces a far different overall picture than the one generally presented by authors and historians in past published accounts.

In the evening of 4 April 1917 Maj Bettington had posted on his unit's notice board the squadron's first-ever operational order, for three separate patrols to be mounted next morning for reconnaissance sorties over the general area of Douai, directly across the trench lines from

Below:
Capt W. L. Robinson VC of No 48 Squadron RFC, in 1917.

Top:
F2A A3343 which was shot down on 5 April 1917 by Manfred von Richthofen for his claimed 36th victory. The crew was Lts H. T. Adams and D. J. Steward of No 48 Squadron RFC.

Above:
F2A A3322 '5' of No 48 Squadron, crewed by 2/Lts R. S. Worsley and H. D. Davis, which was claimed by Lt Lothar von Richthofen Jagdstaffel 11 on 13 April 1917.

Above:
F2B A7195, of the first F2B production batch went to No 48 Squadron RFC and was lost in action on 25 April 1917, with its crew, 2/Lts W. J. Clifford and H. L. Tomkies, both killed.

Bellevue airfield. April 5 dawned in misty weather, but shortly after 09.00hrs the first patrol — six F2As led by Capt W. L. Robinson VC — left base. About the same hour a *kette* (sub-flight) of five Albatros D.IIIs from Jagdstaffel 11 led by Manfred von Richthofen took off from Douai. Shortly after 10.00hrs von Richthofen spotted the Bristols and, as yet unseen by the F2A crews, led his *kette* into attack. (No 48 Squadron's after-combat reports quoted '12 enemy aircraft attacked' but von Richthofen's personal reports mentioned only five of his aircraft actually attacking the F2As.) Selecting the rearmost F2A, A3340 (2/Lt A. N. Leckler and Lt H. D. K. George), as his own victim, the 'Red Knight's' fire was deadly accurate, seriously wounding both men and sending the F2A down to a shaky landing. Both crewmen got out of their F2A and, obeying their strict orders, set fire to the aircraft. Having despatched one victim, von Richthofen next chased after A3343 (Lts H. T. Adams and D. Stewart). Riddling this F2A with bullets and wounding Adams, he forced the Bristol down in German territory where it too was set ablaze by its crew.

Meanwhile the remaining four Bristol crews were in serious trouble as these became engaged by the other four Albatros scouts at very close

Author's Note: 'Albatroses' has been used as the plural of the German 'Aebatros'. RFC usage at the time was 'Albatri'.

quarters. All semblance of tight formation had been lost when the Albatroses had made their initial surprise attack, and each F2A was now fighting alone. Robinson and his gunner, 2/Lt E. D. Warburton, in F2A A3327, attacked one Albatros which promptly spun down (and was later claimed by one F2A survivor as 'Out of control'), but was then attacked by Vizefeldwebel Sebastian Festner, whose fire damaged Robinson's engine, leaving him no alternative but to force-land in enemy territory. A fourth F2A, A3320, manned by Lts L. H. A. Cooper and A. Boldison, came under attack by Leutnant Simon and was quickly shot down. Of the two remaining F2As, one crewed by Lt Pike and 2/Lt H. B. Griffith sent one Albatros spinning down which they later claimed as 'Out of control', then, having completely lost contact with the other Bristol, flew back to base, fighting off two further onslaughts and claiming a further Albatros as 'Driven down'. Thus of the six F2As which set out under Robinson's leadership, four had been shot down, but three Albatros scouts had been *claimed* as either 'Out of control' or 'Driven down' — claims which would seem to discount the popular legend that the F2As' guns had 'frozen' et al. In fact, none of the Albatros scouts had been actually shot down, though their manoeuvres in avoiding being shot at could easily have been misinterpreted by the inexperienced F2A surviving crews.

The second F2A patrol, led by Capt Wilkinson, took off later in the morning and engaged three enemy aircraft near Douai, claiming one as 'Out of control' and a second 'Driven down', then later in the patrol attacked a lone enemy aircraft which was also claimed as 'Driven down'. Wilkinson's

Above:
F2B '2' of No 11 Squadron — named *Rickadamdoo* — and its usual crew, Lts A. P. MacLean (pilot) and George Canthon. Note the gunner's twin yoked Lewis guns. The sloping white bars to either side of the roundel were No 11 Squadron's official marking until 22 March 1918. *A. P. MacLean*

patrol then returned to base without loss or further incident. The third patrol on 5 April was led by Capt D. M. Tidmarsh, and engaged a German two-seater east of Douai, but the enemy pilot managed to escape into nearby cloud cover. Continuing the patrol the F2As next spotted an enemy aircraft southeast of Douai and Lt O. W. Berry promptly engaged this machine, driving it down in a steep spiral. Then Lt G. N. Brockhurst dived on a single red-painted German scout and drove it down, though without positive result.

While available evidence suggests that the losses incurred on 5 April by Robinson's flight were indeed due partly to inexperience and, no doubt, in part to adherence to standard two-seater tactics, it should be noted that claims were made (in good faith) for three enemy aircraft sent down 'Out of control' and a further five 'Driven down' throughout the whole day's actions; indication that at least some crews were more offensive-minded than has been credited in the past. This offensive attitude was borne out in the succeeding weeks. On 6 April, for example, Lt F. P. Holliday and his gunner, Capt A. H. Wall, attacked an enemy aircraft northeast of Arras and apparently shot or killed its pilot; while on the same patrol 2/Lts W. T. Price and Benjamin drove down one German aircraft near Douai 'Out of control', then forced a second to land hastily in a ploughed field. For the Holliday-Wall team this was the first of six enemy aircraft destroyed and eight others claimed as 'Out of control' to fall to their guns over the following 11 weeks. On 7 April the squadron suffered another casualty when one F2A returned with a dead Observer, 2/Lt G. C. Burnard, but on the following day the 'balance' was to a great extent restored when a F2A patrol tackled a larger enemy formation and claimed two as 'Out of control' and four others 'Driven down', for the loss of F2A A3330, which was crewed by 2/Lts O. W. Berry and F. B. Goodison who were apparently victims of Leutnant Otto Bernert of Jagdstaffel *Boelcke* and were both killed.

April 9 saw plentiful action for No 48 Squadron. Capt Wilkinson and Lt H. B. Griffiths opened the day's 'accounts' by destroying a two-seater near Lens, then sent an Albatros two-seater down 'Out of control' for good measure. 2/Lt W. T. Price and 2/Lt Benjamin in another F2A destroyed an enemy aircraft east of Arras on the same sortie. On his second patrol the same day Capt Wilkinson, with Lt L. W. Allen now in the rear cockpit, joined forces with a second F2A (Lts J. H. Letts and Collins) in attacking five enemy aircraft near Arras, destroying one and shooting a second down 'Out of control'. Unfortunately, Letts' gunner, Lt H. G. Collins, was killed in this action, while back at base 2/Lt A. B. Anstey was seriously injured in an accident. Two days later, on 11 April, a formation of four F2As had the misfortune to run into a gaggle of Albatros D.IIIs from von Richthofen's Jagdstaffel 11. Despite later claims

by surviving F2A crews for one German 'shot down' and two others as 'Out of control', three F2As failed to return. A3338 (Capt D. M. Tidmarsh and 2/Lt C. B. Holland) fell victim to Leutnant Kurt Wolff; A3323 (2/Lts G. N. Brockhurst and C. B. Broughton) was brought down by the 'Red Knight's' younger brother, Leutnant Lothar von Richthofen; while the third loss was A3318 (2/Lts R. E. Adeney and L. G. Lovell). Such losses did not impair the squadron's offensive spirit, as exemplified on the following day when a pair of F2As (Capt Wilkinson and Lt L. W. Allen, and 2/Lts O. B. Winkler and E. S. Moore) calmly tackled a formation of seven enemy aircraft and sent one down 'Out of control'.

April 13 proved particularly unlucky for 2/Lts R. S. Worsley and H. D. Davis, flying F2A A3322 '5', when they were claimed as shot down by Leutnant Lothar von Richthofen to become prisoners of war, and 'presented' the Germans with an intact example of their new aircraft. Their loss was quickly avenged 24 hours later when Capt Wilkinson and Lt Allen, and Lts Warren and Smith coolly took on a formation of 20 enemy aircraft, and destroyed one, then sent a second down 'Out of control'. Their keenness to tackle the enemy, no matter what the odds, was further demonstrated on 22 April when a F2A patrol engaged 14 enemy aircraft and Capt Wilkinson and Lt Allen shot one down 'Out of control', while two others were claimed as 'Driven down' — and again without loss to the Bristol crews. The next day saw an F2A patrol tackle a formation of 10 enemy aircraft over Vitry. The team of Holliday and Wall quickly destroyed one, and the rest of the patrol claimed two others as 'Out of control' and 'Driven down, severely damaged'; the F2As' only casualty was Lt L. E. Porter wounded. Holliday and Wall added another German destroyed near Cagnicourt on 24 April, as well as a second 'Out of control'; while on 25 April Lts W. T. Price and Benjamin also claimed a German aircrft destroyed. The same day, however, 2/Lts W. J. Clifford and H. L. Tomkies were killed in acton in A7195. Claims were made on two more occasions before the end of the month. On 27 April Lt Price and Benjamin sent a two-seater down to crash into the River Scarpe, near Vitry; and on 30 April a F2A reconnaissance patrol had several separate combats, in the course of which two enemy aircraft were claimed as 'Out of control', but one crew, Lt H. C. Patterson and Cpl R. Edwards, were killed. Thus, in its first 26 days of operations, No 48 Squadron had lost totals of 11 aircraft, 24 men killed or prisoner of war, and two others wounded, but had claimed totals of nine enemy aircraft confirmed as destroyed, 18 others as 'Out of control', plus a further 13 'Driven down'. In the arithmetic of war, such figures indicate a 'profit' clearly in favour of the Bristol crews.

By then No 48 Squadron's crews, still the only Bristol Fighter crews on operations in France, had begun evolving new tactics for their aircraft, with pilots becoming increasingly confident in flying their aircraft as virtual single-seat fighters, using the forward gun to good advantage, and as experience between individual two-men 'teams' deepened an intuitive understanding between pilot and gunner raised the efficiency of both in defence and/or offence in combat, the leading exemplars being the Holliday/Wall duo in this context. This new comprehension of the aircraft's full potential was put to good effect during May 1917, commencing on 2 May when 2/Lts H. C. Farnes and Davis shot an Albatros two-seater down 'Out of control' during an early patrol. That evening a second patrol encountered a formation of 10 red Albatros D.IIIs and promptly attacked. In the ensuing combat Lts Winkler and Moore destroyed one Albatros and sent a second 'Out of control'; 2/Lts Harrison and Richards, despite both being wounded, shot one Albatros down 'Out of control'; Lts Scholte and Game destroyed a fourth Albatros in flames; and two others were at least damaged and driven down. On 4 May Capt J. H. Letts and Lt Smither shot a German aircraft down to crash near Pelves, and three days later three enemy aircraft were claimed as 'Forced to land' — moral, if not necessarily positive, victories. On 9 May the redoubtable team of Holliday and Wall joined 2/Lts Price and Moore in attacking two enemy aircraft near Vitry, forcing one of these down to land in a field, whereupon both Bristol crews strafed its occupants. That evening a F2A patrol engaged eight German aircraft near Vitry, with Holliday and Wall claiming two as 'Out of control' and 2/Lt W. T. Price and C. G. Clay crashing a third, despite being both wounded and the shot down in A7110.

Left and below:
Two views of No 11 Squadron F2B's rear gun defence. Note the extended exhaust pipes.
A. P. MacLean Collection

May 10 saw Lt T. P. Middleton and 2/Lt Malcolmson engage 10 enemy scouts and shoot one down to crash, but during the day two officers were killed in action (2/Lts G. E. Hawkesley and L. Speller). The next day brought more casualties when a No 48 Squadron patrol clashed with 12 Albatros scouts. Holliday and Wall destroyed one Albatros and sent a second tumbling down, hopelessly out of control, while two other Bristol crews jointly despatched a third Albatros 'Out of control'. Two Bristols were, however, lost — A7101 (Capt A. T. Coll and Lt E. S. Moore killed) and A7111 (2/Lt O. B. Winkler and LAM A. T. Russon, also both killed), while 2/Lt F. M. Magenais received wounds. On 20 May, while on an escort sortie, the Bristols were jumped by a much larger number of German scout aircraft and had several running combats, in the course of which 2/Lt Fraser/Pte J. H. Muscott shot one German fighter down with its tail section broken, and two other Bristols combined to shoot down two Germans 'Out of control'. One Bristol, A3341 (2/Lts J. A. Armstrong and G. Baines) failed to return. Four days later Capt J. H. Letts and Lt L. W. Allen attacked a quartet of German two-seaters, shooting one down 'Out of control', severely damaging a second, and forcing the remaining pair to flee eastwards, though Allen was wounded during the proceedings. On 27 May 2/Lt T. P. Middleton and his Observer, 2/LT A. W. Merchant, were set upon by three Albatros scouts, but destroyed one of these and drove off its companions; then later in the same patrol they engaged a two-seater and left it spinning to earth out of control. The evening patrol on that date had something of a field-day when it closed with a formation of Germans just south of Douai and accounted for one destroyed and four others claimed as 'Out of control'; their only casualty was 2/Lt G. Barnes, who was wounded. The squadron's 'balance sheet' for May

This page:
Three progressive views of F2B A7231 '1' of 'A' Flight, No 11 Squadron RFC (Lts Scholz and Wookey) after being shot down on 17 October 1917 by Vzfw Bey of Jasta 5. *All: A. E. Ferko*

1917 amounted to four Bristols lost in action, 10 men killed or 'missing', and five wounded in combat, as against claims for nine enemy aircraft confirmed as destroyed, 18 others as 'Out of control', with six more either 'driven down' or forced to land.

If further evidence was required of No 48 Squadron's crews' confidence in their warhorses and their offensive tactics, a glance at the unit's 'tally' for the following period of 1 June to 7 July shows the Bristol crews claiming totals of nine destroyed and 11 'Out of control' against unit casualties of two Bristols and their crews shot down and four men wounded in action. Particularly noteworthy during that period was an engagement in the evening of 15 June. The doughty team of Holliday and Wall were flying a lone patrol when they spotted a force of seven German fighters. Knowing that a patrol from their own unit was due any minute from the north, Holliday acted as decoy 'bait' to draw the German formation after him, and as the other Bristols appeared a milling dogfight quickly ensued. Holliday and Wall fastened on to one German's tail and shot him down 'Out of control', while two other Bristols — Lts Pratt and Owen and Lts Fraser and Benjamin — combined to send a second down 'Out of control'. A further 'pairing' — Capt Baker and Lt Munro, and Lt Binnie and LAM Reed — concentrated their fire on one German which fell away streaming a plume of flames; then Binnie and Reed switched quickly to another target and left the German falling totally out of control. Finally Lts R. B. Hay and Nutkins caught one German unawares and destroyed him.

Among other examples of the Bristol crews' offensive spirit was a patrol on 18 June when 2/Lt T. P. Middleton and Lt A. W. Merchant calmly attacked alone a formation of seven enemy aircraft and destroyed one before the remainder scattered for safety; while on 3 July the Holliday/Wall duo tackled five German aircraft and claimed one as 'Out of control' to add to the squadron's 'bag' of two more 'Out of control' claims and one destroyed throughout that day's actions. On 6 July, however, after five weeks of action without a single aircraft lost in combat, a No 48 Squadron patrol ran into a formation of Albatros fighters from Jagdstaffel 3, losing A7137 (2/Lt H. Smither and H. C. Clarke) in flames, and A7109 (2/Lt H. C. Farnes and Cpl J. T. Park) to the wheeling Albatroses. Lt Scholte and A. W. Merchant destroyed one German and Capt J. T. Milne and 2/Lt Tanner claimed a second as 'Out of control'. On the following day Capt J. T. Milne and 2/Lt A. D. Light shot down one German which crashed in a wood near Vitry, while 2/Lts Elliott and Ferguson claimed another as 'Out of control'.

In summary, for the whole period of 5 April to 7 July 1917 — 94 days — No 48 Squadron had suffered overall totals of 17 aircraft and 36 men lost in action, with 13 other crewmen wounded to some degree. In balance the crews had claimed a total of 93 enemy aircraft destroyed, 'Out of control' or driven down — almost exactly one enemy aircraft rendered hors de combat for every day of flying. The unit's casualty figures represented virtually a normal squadron establishment of men and machines, yet this was by no means an uncommon casualty rate at the period in question; April 1917 — later to be grimly termed 'Bloody April' — had been the RFC's worst-ever month of the aerial war in the context of losses, and No 48 Squadron's crews had been truly 'blooded' in that month, mostly facing death in the air for the first time, and flying newly introduced and 'untested' aircraft with almost no comparative precedents to guide them in terms of tactics. By comparison with other 'fighter' squadrons during those fateful weeks — units well versed in aerial warfare and flying well-tried and familiar aircraft — No 48 Squadron had proved itself the equal of any veteran unit in achievement, courage and offensive spirit.

By the close of June 1917 No 48 Squadron had ceased to be the only Bristol Fighter unit in France. At its base, Bellevue, No 11 Squadron, an FE2b reconnaissance unit, began receiving Bristol Fighters during early June and by the 13th was sufficiently re-equipped on its new machines to commence operations with these. Commanded then by Maj C. T. Maclean, No 11 already possessed a distinguished fighting record with its former Vickers FB5 and FE aircraft, and its crews were mostly veterans of aerial warfare over the Western Front. With No 48 Squadron's example in mind, No 11 Squadron's Bristol crews looked eagerly towards using their new machines in action, and adopted 48's attitude of flying the Bristols primarily as fighters. The unit's first casualties in action occurred on 21 June when Bristol Fighter A7139 (2/Lt D. C. MacBrayne and Sgt W. Mollison) was last seen at 06.45hrs going down in enemy territory, but other crews quickly familiarised themselves with the new techniques required in fighting the Bristols, and on 26 June a patrol from No 11 Squadron clashed with 10 enemy fighters. Two Germans attacked a Bristol crewed by Lt Andrew McKeever and 2/Lt E. Oake from behind but the Canadian pilot swiftly retaliated, sending one down 'Out of control', then tackled a third German fighter which McKeever destroyed. In another Bristol Lt G. H. Hooper and Cpl Carr destroyed one German scout, while 2/Lt P. C. Ross and 2/AM Woodward engaged four Germans, destroying one and shooting down a second 'Out of control' before Ross, seriously wounded, left the fight and returned to land safely at base, only to die later from his wounds. Next day 2/Lts Hytch and McRobert attacked a large two-seater near Monchy and drove it down out of control to crash.

Andrew Edward McKeever, born in Listowel, Ontario on 21 August 1895, had transferred from the Army to the RFC, and gained his pilot's wings on 6 December 1916. On 16 May 1917 he joined No 11 Squadron to begin a war career with this squadron (ending on 26 January 1918 when he returned to England) which would see him claim a total of 30 combat victories and be awarded a DSO, MC and Bar, and Croix de Guerre — all in Bristol Fighters, thereby making McKeever the highest-scoring two-seater fighting pilot in any air service of the 1914-18 conflict. His victory on 26 June was his third accredited enemy aircraft destroyed, and by 11 July his tally had risen to eight, resulting in his first Military Cross decoration. By the end of August he had added a Bar to his MC (Gazetted 27 October 1917), and at the end of November came the award of a DSO. A typical example of McKeever's early prowess in the Bristol Fighter came on 8 July when, with 2/Lt A. L. Powell manning the rear cockpit, McKeever dived on one German aircraft and shot it down to crash, then attacked a second and sent this down out of control. He next tackled four Germans and his accurate shooting shot down one of these hopelessly out of control. That evening another No 11 Squadron patrol attacked 16 German aircraft near Bohain, resulting in two Germans being claimed as 'Out of control' by the duos Capt Raymond-Barker and Pte J. Mason and 2/Lts A. J. Hytch and McRobert. On 10 July the unit scored again, when 2/Lts F. J. Foster and H. J. Day met an Albatros scout over Lecluse and sent it down to crash with a burst of 50 rounds. A second German was destroyed near Gouelzin by 2/Lt Sharples and 2/AM Bassenger, while a third was shot down out of control by McKeever and 2/Lt W. Dodd. Four days later, still with Dodd as his Observer/gunner, McKeever attacked three enemy aircraft, driving two down and the third 'Out of control'.

In the late morning of 22 July, two Bristols from No 48 Squadron had an unusual victory. Based by then at Bray Dunes, Capt Brian E. Baker (Observer, 2/Lt G. R. Spencer) in A7146 was patrolling at some 16,000ft when he spotted five German Gotha bombers very low down about eight miles northwest of Ostend. Baker immediately dived to attack, being joined by Lt R. D. Coath and 2/Lt A. D. Merchant in A7164. Attacking from the beam at 3,000ft, Baker saw his tracers hitting his selected Gotha in its nose section, while Coath attacked the same bomber from its rear. The huge bomber continued diving and eventually crashed in the sea just off Ostende in shallow waters, remaining with its upper wing awash and its tail unit showing clear of the surface. It had been returning from a raid on Southend and Harwich, and was subsequently classified in German records as 'Crashed on landing'. . . .! Brian Baker was to become commander of No 141 Squadron RAF (Bristol F2Bs) at Biggin Hill in 1918, and eventually rose in RAF service to become Air Marshal Sir Brian Baker KBE, CB, DSO, MC, AFC.

Above:

Fighting Canucks. Majors D. R. McLaren DSO, MC, DFC (54 victories) and (right) Andrew E. McKeever DSO, MC (30 victories in F2Bs), at Upper Heyford in 1918.

Public Archives of Canada: PA-6023

Even as No 11 Squadron was getting into its stride in its new Bristols, a third unit began slowly converting to the type — No 22 Squadron, based at Boisdinghem from 14 August 1917 under the command of Maj L. W. Learmount. A former FE2b unit, No 22 Squadron began receiving some Bristol F2Bs in late July and by mid-August had completed replacement of all FEs. The majority of No 22 Squadron's aircrews were at that time reasonably fresh to the operational scene in France, while the new aircraft arrived as final preparations were being made to launch the Third Battle of Ypres. Even the more experienced ex-FE2b pilots needed to adjust themselves in large measure to the Bristol F2B, which not only

Below:
An F2B of No 11 Squadron taxying out for a sortie. *A. P. MacLean Collection*

reversed the pilot/gunner locations from those in an FE, but also placed the pilot behind the engine. The F2B's superior performance over the FE created fresh conditions too, particularly its greater fighting ceiling and consequent need for more physical stamina in the thinner, less-oxygenated air of 15-18,000ft altitudes on occasion. Added to such items were the various purely technical problems of coping with new Vickers guns, new engines, new rigging and structural maintenance which collectively gave a number of 'teething' headaches to air and ground crews during 22's first few months employing F2Bs. One of the squadron's first patrols in F2Bs took off on 11 August, led by Capt C. M. Clement and Pte Clement, and clashed with six Albatros scouts northeast of Douai. Though one Albatros was shot down in flames, and a second sent down out of control, two F2Bs were lost — A7179 (Lts E. A. H. Ward and K. W. Holmes) and A7169 (Capt P. W. Chambers and 2/AM W. Richman) — while one pilot, Lt R. N. Treadwell MC, was wounded.

Clement's flight avenged these losses two days later when he led his men against a formation of seven Albatroses, destroying one in flames and shooting down three others out of control, without loss to the F2Bs, but on 19 August, flying A7172, Clement, with Lt R. B. Carter as gunner, was himself shot down in flames. Clement had by then served with No 22 Squadron continuously for some 14 months — as in all warfare, sheer experience was no guarantee against death in combat. Even as the No 22 Squadron crews wrestled with the various problems of fighting in F2Bs, No 48 Squadron was demonstrating only too clearly the full potential of their aircraft. On 17 August, for merely one example, a No 48 Squadron patrol had a hectic time, with a series of fights against heavy odds in numbers. One such clash saw 2/Lt Keith Park and A. Noss destroy two enemy scouts and shoot down two others out of control; while two other F2Bs combined to attack a fifth Albatros which literally fell apart in mid-air under their fire, and a sixth German was shot down to crash near Ostend by the crew, Sgt W. Roebuck and 2/AM W. Walker. Keith Park was later to rise to Major and command No 48 Squadron from April to November 1918, and rose thereafter in RAF service to become Air Chief Marshal Sir Keith Park GCB, KBE, MC, DFC, DCL. Yet another example of No 48 Squadron's prowess occurred on 22 August when five F2Bs engaged 20 enemy aircraft over Ghistelles aerodrome and accounted for six of these either destroyed (three) or out of control.

Despite occasional victory claims, No 22 Squadron was suffering relatively serious casualties; as on 23 August when one German aircraft was claimed 'Out of control' but the unit lost two F2Bs — A7204 (2/Lt H. G. Tambling and F/Sgt W. Organ) and B1101 (Sgt C. L. Randell/1AM J. V. Hurley) — with a third pilot wounded. In September 1917 the squadron's casualty toll increased with eight men killed and six others wounded, including the crews of F2Bs A7149 and A7233 which collided in the air killing all four crew men. At this period particularly No 22 Squadron was short of sufficient trained Observer-gunners and no few F2B rear cockpits were being occupied by volunteers from the unit's ground maintenance air mechanics — indeed, eight of the squadron's casualties in August-September had been non-commissioned personnel. In the words of one ex-No 22 Squadron pilot: 'A picture which survives in the minds of some from those days is of the squadron ambulance bucketing across the grass-land to collect the dead and wounded from machines which straggled back, some in serious condition simply from loss of blood, which the provision of first aid kits in the machines could have reduced in some cases'. (*Pi in the Sky* by W. Harvey; C. Huston, 1971.)

On 10 September 1917 No 22 Squadron moved base to Estree Blanche airfield, south of St Omer, in preparation for the Battle of Menin Road Ridge (Ypres) due to be launched on 20 September. Only a week before No 22 Squadron's move yet another Bristol F2B unit commenced operations on the type when No 20 Squadron, based at St Marie Cappelle under the command of Maj W. H. C. Mansfield, claimed its first victim in the F2B. An FE2d unit, No 20 Squadron had begun receiving F2B replacements in late August 1917 but continued to fly a mixture of FE and F2B patrols. Then, on 3 September, four FE2ds of the squadron engaged on a photo-recce sortie were jumped by a dozen German scouts. As the fight evolved four Bristol F2Bs from the same squadron arrived and 2/Lt R. Makepeace and Lt E. Waddington shot down one Albatros scout to crash — the squadron's first in F2Bs. On 11 September the squadron sent off a formation of six F2Bs for a photo-recce but these became engaged by some 25 German scouts near Menin. 'With their customary vigorousness of attack . . .' — as the day's RFC communique termed it — the F2Bs promptly shot down two Germans in flames, and two others out of control. Later the same day another F2B patrol shot down a fifth near Wervicq. One pilot who scored that day was Lt H. G. E. Luchford in F2B A7248, who was eventually to be credited with at least 24 combat victories before his death at the hands of Leutnant Walter von Bülow of Jagdstaffel 36 on 2 December 1917. On 19 September one F2B crew — 2/Lts A. G. V. Taylor and H. Dandy in A7246 — set out on a lone photo-recce sortie, crossed the trench-lines, and Dandy in the rear cockpit began operating his camera. As he crouched in his cockpit eight Albatroses attacked the F2B, the first to do so wounding Dandy seriously in a leg. Ignoring his wound, Dandy promptly returned fire sending one Albatros spinning down in flames and two others out of control. As a pause in the onslaught came, Dandy told Taylor of his wound and when the pilot looked around he saw that the F2B's tail section was almost severed from the fuselage. By careful handling Taylor nursed the crippled F2B back to safety. In his combat report Taylor made a point of mentioning that Dandy had fought the Albatroses *after* being wounded — only to have the squadron commander pencil on a cryptic comment 'Why not?'.

Inevitably perhaps, No 22 Squadron's crews suffered casualties as they adapted their techniques to the Bristol Fighter. On 21 September F2B A7234 (Lts C. H. C. Woods and F. W. MacLean) was shot down by a Jagdstaffel 29 pilot (either Leutnant Herman Göring or Leutnant Kieckhafer, both of whom claimed Bristol F2B victims from this combat), and on 28 September two formations of four F2Bs each ran into about 25 Albatros scouts near Menin. In the desperate fight which ensued Lt Luchford and 2/Lt R. F. Hill in B1122 claimed two Albatroses as destroyed, but A7210 (Capt J. S. Campbell and Driver G. Tester) was shot down by Leutnant Josef Veltjens, and A7241 (Lts H. F. Tomlin and T. H. Noble) was sent down in flames by Oberleutnant Harold Auffarth; both Germans being from Jagdstaffel 18. In early October Maj E. H. Johnston became 20's latest commander, and throughout the month 20's crews were to claim a total of 27 victories, with Luchford as the most prominent scorer. Nevertheless casualties continued to mount. On the 5 October Oberleutnant Erwin Böhme of Jagdstaffel Bölcke claimed the crew of Capt D. D. W. Skinner and Pte F. J. Johns for his 16th *luftsieg*; while on 8 October F2B B1125 (Lt W. D. Chambers and 2/Lt F. H. Berry) was forced to land on the airfield of Fl-Abt.A217. On 15 October another F2B crew, Lts J. P. Dalley and L. H. Gould, became prisoners of war, and two days later A7271 went down in flames bearing Lts A. G. V. Taylor and Sgt W. J. Benger MM to their deaths.

While Nos 11, 20, 22 and 48 Squadrons continued to embellish the Bristol F2B's fighting record along the Western Front in France, F2Bs were already equipping other RFC units based in England. No 62 Squadron, originally formed at Netheravon on 28 July 1916, was finally mobilised for operations in France in May 1917 and began receiving F2Bs for this purpose, but to the dismay of its eager crews the order was rescinded shortly after and the squadron remained a training unit, producing Bristol F2B pilots for service in France, until being re-mobilised in October 1917 at Rendcombe under the command of a new OC, Maj Frank W. Smith, from 18 October. The long wait for 'foreign' service for No 62 Squadron eventually ended in January 1918 when various parties, ground and air, crossed the Channel to France. A second unit destined for France was No 88 Squadron which originally formed at

Above:
F2B E2601 'H' of No 22 Squadron (pilot, Lt J. E. White). This F2B was the ultimate F2B flown back to England when No 22 Squadron returned from France after the armistice.

Above:
F2B B1153 of No 22 Squadron (2/Lts A. F. Goodchap and A. H. Middleton), which was shot down by ground fire on 3 December 1917. *A. E. Ferko*

Gosport on 24 July 1917 and was soon equipped with Bristol F2Bs, but only arrived in France ultimately on 20 April 1918. A third UK-based unit to receive Bristol F2Bs was No 39 Squadron, a home defence unit based at Woodford primarily in September 1917 when its first F2Bs began arriving to replace its antiquated BE 'fighters'. It had been with No 39 Squadron that Capt W. L. Robinson — of No 48 Squadron in April 1917 — had won his Victoria Cross in September 1916. No 39's Bristols were destined to see little action during the following year, and in October 1918 the squadron was transferred to France, based at Bavichove, but again saw no action before the armistice.

The final two months of operations in France during 1917 for the F2B squadrons, and indeed the RFC in general, were hectic. While aerial combat with the opposing German jagdstaffeln predominated in most communiques and other records, the Bristol crews of all units undertook a variety of other, less spectacular but perhaps more important, duties. Escorting de Havilland 4 day bombers deep into German territory usually meant plentiful aerial opposition on both outward and return flights; the latter almost invariably against strong westerly winds, with depleting fuel supply, and beset by would-be German interceptor fighters. On such escort duties the value of the F2B rear gunners was enhanced by holding close formations and combining their fire-power with that of the DH4s' rear defenders. Photographic reconnaissance was more or less a permanent feature of the F2B squadrons' daily routine — often flown by merely single or paired aircraft and just as often fiercely challenged by German fighter formations. Other roles included very low-level ground-strafing 'shoots' of German first-line trench systems with all the hazards involved of murderous ground-fire, tree-stumps, passing artillery shells, and ever-present risks of fatal collisions during any concentrated operations by several units.

A case in point was the opening of the Battle of Cambrai on 20 November when the British 1st and

3rd Armies launched a new offensive south and southwest of Cambrai. Weather conditions were appalling, with very low cloud and dense mists, but the RFC flew to its limits in support of the PBI ('Poor Bloody Infantry'). All RFC units involved flew bombing, strafing and general recce sorties at near-suicidal heights over the raging battle scenes below. Few enemy aircraft were met initially — some German unit commanders refusing to order their pilots to fly at all in such weather — but the RFC aircraft maintained their efforts despite driving rain and almost nil visibility on occasion. On 23 November a No 11 Squadron F2B crew, 2/Lt Rivers and Lt Podgson, sent one German aircraft down totally out of control — the 100th enemy aircraft claimed by this squadron since exchanging its FE2Bs for Bristol F2Bs; but such combats were relatively rare during the opening phase of the ground offensive. On 30 November, however, the redoubtable F2B duo, Capt Andrew McKeever and Lt L. A. Powell of No 11 Squadron, had a remarkably successful confrontation with nine German Albatros scouts, resulting in each man destroying two enemy aircraft. The first victim fell to McKeever who fired at 15yd range and sent it down in flames, then Powell shot two more down despite suffering a stoppage in his Lewis gun during the fighting. The fourth Albatros made the mistake of over-shooting the F2B and was promptly shot down by McKeever. The fight was a prolonged struggle, in the course of which McKeever fought within 20ft of the ground and eventually pretended that he was about to land before suddenly giving his engine full boost and zooming away out of range of the remaining Albatros.

December 1917 saw a continuance of bad weather conditions for most of the month, but the F2Bs flew whenever possible, carrying out general reconnaissance sorties, escort patrols and occasional OPs (Offensive Patrols, ie pure fighting 'hunts' for German aircraft). They reaped relatively few victims compared with previous months, although occasional flare-ups in the air war occurred, as on 5 December when F2B crews of No 20 Squadron accounted for three German aircraft in combats, while No 22 Squadron claimed two others destroyed. Casualties among the F2B crews were not small; No 22 Squadron alone lost two F2Bs and crews to enemy action, four other aircraft and their crews killed or injured in flying accidents, and one crewman who died of his wounds. During its first nine months of operations in France, albeit in relatively small numbers initially, the Bristol Fighter had established itself conclusively as the best two-seat fighter on the Western Front from any viewpoint and had long given the lie to Manfred von Richthofen's personal assessment of the design after his first F2A victories in April; 'It appears to be quick and handy . . . (but) the D.III Albatros was, both in speed and ability to climb, undoubtedly superior'. (*The Red Knight of Germany*, by F. Gibbons; Cassell, 1930.)

Below:
F2B B1125 of No 20 Squadron RFC (2/Lts F. H. Berry and Lt W. D. Chambers) which force-landed on the airfield base of *Flieger-Abteilung A217* on 8 October 1917. After slight repairs, it was re-marked in German colours and flown by German pilots as a 'hack'. *A. E. Ferko*

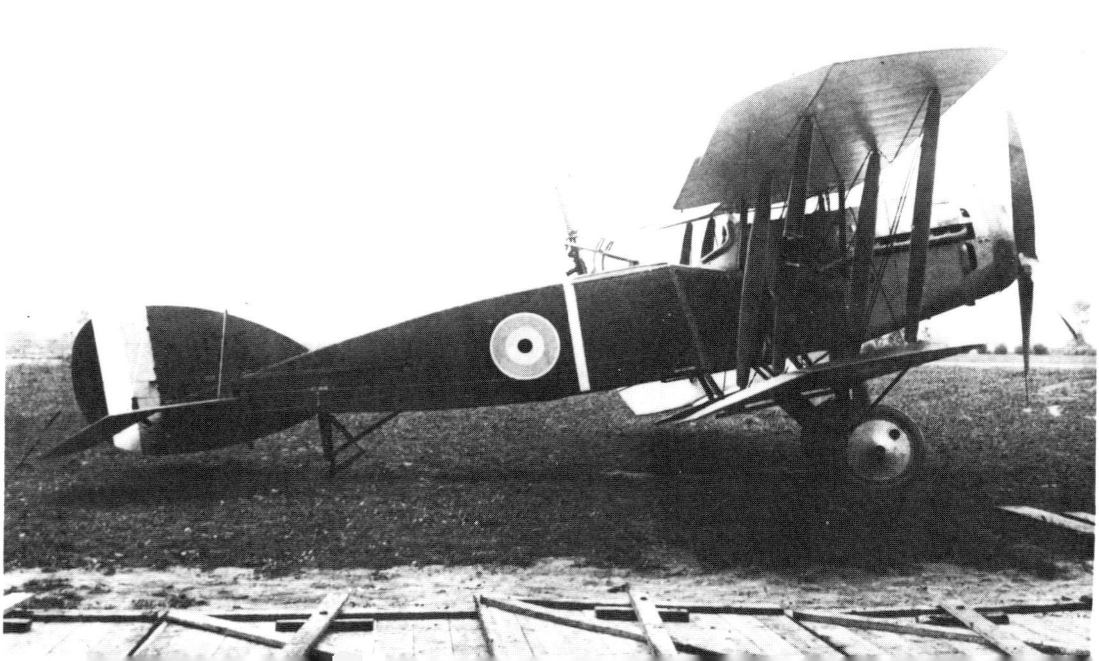

Western Front 1918

Even as the RFC crews were flying through the murk of battle over the Cambrai and Bourlon Wood mud-flats in the closing weeks of 1917, moves were afoot back in England to transform the whole of Britain's flying services into a single force, independently administered and controlled by its own ministry in government. The Air Force Bill, which in turn legally created the Royal Air Force and its Air Ministry, had been introduced in the House of Commons on 8 November 1917. Despite various wranglings and clashes of individual personalities involved, the first Air Council was constituted by an Order in Council of 2 January 1918 and the Air Council became established on the following day, with Lord Rothermere as its president, and Maj-Gen Sir Hugh Trenchard KCB, DSO as the first-ever appointed Chief of the Air Staff (CAS). The actual 'birth' of the new Service, the Royal Air Force, was delayed until 1 April 1918 (a date selected simply to coincide with the start of a fresh financial budgeting year by the Civil Service bureaucracy), when the Royal Naval Air Service (RNAS) and Royal Flying Corps (RFC) were amalgamated to form the Third Service. Though there were to be further disagreements and personality clashes among the various political and Service personnel in London over the projected new Service, the RAF duly celebrated its 'birthday' on April Fools' Day.

To the fighting airmen in France these machinations in the power corridors of 'Bolo House' (the RFC airmen's cynical nickname for Hotel Cecil, London, home of RFC HQ) were unknown as the new year commenced. The recent battles had been bloodily costly to both German and Allied armies and their respective air services, and all were busy replenishing material strength and replacing personnel casualties. Weather conditions in early January 1918 nullified aerial action on any large scale, but the opposing air forces maintained their daily and nightly support of their ground forces whenever possible. During 1-7 January the RFC claimed totals of 24 enemy aircraft destroyed and eight others 'Out of control', for the losses of 11 RFC aircraft reported as 'Missing'; but much of RFC aerial activity was not concerned with air combat, concentrating mainly on bombing raids and — as ever — daily photo-reconnaissance over the German lines. It was on one such 'camera-job' on 1 January that 2/Lt Chick and Lt Kincaird of No 11 Squadron opened the F2Bs' 1918 account by attacking a German scout and shooting it down out of control. Two days later, while engaged in another photo-recce, 2/Lts W. Beaver and H. E. Easton in F2B B883, along with three other F2Bs, spotted an Albatros two-seater northeast of Moorslede, dived on it, fired 50 rounds from close range, and saw the Albatros crash and erupt in flames. On the same day Capt Keith Park and Lt J. Robertson of No 48 Squadron, engaged on a photo-recce sortie, were attacked by six German scouts. Despite damage to Park's engine, they succeeded in shooting one German down out of control and then evaded further attacks. Next day No 20 Squadron claimed two more victims during a series of combats while on reconnaissance patrols, one of these from a batch of five Albatroses which attacked F2B A7255 (2/Lt R. M. Makepeace MC and Capt J. H. Hedley). The next few days brought snowstorms, mist and low cloud bases, restricting aerial activity to a great degree, but the F2Bs continued their recce sorties and claimed several enemy aircraft shot down in the process.

The closing weeks of January 1918 brought heavy rainstorms over the Western Front yet aerial activity steadily increased, with a consequent rise in the number of clashes with enemy aircraft. On 22 January, for example, No 20 Squadron sent off a patrol of 11 F2Bs to seek out German aircraft. The patrol was attacked by 20 Albatroses and in the melee which followed 2/Lts D. G. Cooke and H. G. Crowe (A7256) shot one Albatros down out of control, then a second in flames; Capt R. K. Kirkman and 2/AM J. McMechan (B1156) sent one Albatros down out of control; and Sgt H. O. Smith and 2/Lt C. J. Agelasto (B883) shot a fourth Albatros down to crash. Three days later, on

Right:
F2B C4630 of No 62 Squadron ('J') before and after being shot down on 19 May 1918 (2/Lt H. A.Clarke and Capt H. Claye); this victory was credited to Lt Delling of Jasta 34b.

Below:
Also shot down on 19 May 1918 was F2B C4751 'T' of No 62 Squadron (Lt F. Atkinson and Sgt C. Brammer), by Vzfw Kahlow of Jasta 34b. Just visible beyond the F2B are the remains of the Pfalz D. IIIa crashed by Leutnant Bayernfeind of Jasta 34b shortly after the F2B landed. *A. E. Ferko*

25 January, the crews of No 20 Squadron chalked up yet another resounding victory, claiming seven Albatros scouts — five of which were certainly destroyed — from a formation of 12 Albatroses. On 30 January two more victories were claimed by No 20 Squadron crews, but on the same day a F2B from No 22 Squadron was attacked and set afire above the German reserve trenchlines. Its pilot, 2/Lt G. G. Johnson, was killed leaving his gunner, Driver R. A. Duff, to attempt to land the aircraft despite having no flying experience. Duff managed to crash-land the burning F2B but died soon after from his burns and other injuries — a fate all too common among the 'back-seat' crews when their pilots became incapacitated in any way.

In January reinforcement in the shape of No 62 Squadron arrived in France, its transport and ground personnel leaving England by sea on 18 and 21 January respectively, and its Bristol Fighters being flown over on 29 January to St Omer — albeit losing F2B B1246 en route, which ditched in the Channel although its crew was rescued. On 1 February the unit moved to Serny where it came under the aegis of 9th Wing RFC, and its first patrols were flown on 17 January. Four days later Capts G. F. Hughes and H. Claye in C4630 'J' claimed the squadron's first confirmed combat victory when they sent a two-seater down to crash near Armentieres: this particular F2B team was eventually to be credited with at least 11 combat victories between them. On 8 March the squadron moved base again, this time to Cachy, from where it commenced a near-routine of daily Offensive Patrols and claimed eight victories on 10 and 11 March. On 12 March, however, No 62 Squadron clashed with the famed 'Richthofen Circus' — the combined four-staffeln Jagdgeschwader Nr 1 commanded by Rittmeister Manfred von Richthofen — and suffered its first casualties due to direct enemy action. Leaving Cachy at 10am, nine F2Bs on an OP over Cambrai were attacked an hour later by three veteran pilots of Jagdstaffel 11 — Ltn Werner Steinhäuser, Ltn Lothar von Richthofen, and the 'Red Baron' himself flying Fokker Dr1 triplane 152/17. Two of the Bristols had left the patrol to dive on a German two-seater and the trio of Germans chose that moment to engage the F2Bs. The results were four F2Bs falling to the Germans' guns: C4824 (Lt J. H. Ferguson and Sgt D. Lough) to Steinhäuser, B1247 (Capt D. S. Kennedy MC and Lt H. Goddard) to Lothar von Richthofen, which erupted in flames and its two crewmen jumped overboard rather than die in the fire, and B1250 (2/Lt O. B. Fenton and Lt H. P. Boyce) also to Lothar von Richthofen; while Manfred von Richthofen shot down F2B B1251 crewed by 2/Lts C. L. F. Clutterbuck and H. J. Sparks, severely wounding Sparks in the process. Despite these losses, No 62 Squadron was out in strength next day with an OP of 11 F2Bs along a line Cambrai-Le Cateau. Here they again clashed with the 'Circus', only this time the 'Red Knight' was leading a combined formation from JG.1 of some 35 scouts. The F2B formation leaders, Capt G. F. Hughes and H. Claye in C4630, spotted the gaily

Below:

F2B E2459 '12' of No 88 Squadron, usually crewed by Lts F. Jeffries and C. M. B. Martin. Behind (left) is F2B E2458 '8', which also saw service with No 48 Squadron as '9' of that unit.

coloured gaggle of Fokker Triplanes, Albatroses and Pfalz scouts at various altitudes and tried to 'decoy' these into following his formation away from some DH4s of Nos 25 and 27 Squadrons on a bombing raid a few miles away. Hughes succeeded in this ploy, but as he was about to cross back into Allied territory one of his formation dived on some Fokkers below and Hughes had to turn and join the ensuing combat.

Driving a red and green triplane off the tail of one F2B, Hughes next attacked a Pfalz on the tail of a second F2B and shot it down. He next engaged a red-nosed triplane and his Observer, Hugh Claye, sank a burst of 50 rounds into this at 50yd range. The triplane fell away vertically, shedding fabric from its top wing and eventually crashed badly, seriously injuring its pilot, Lothar von Richthofen, who spent many subsequent weeks in a hospital bed — some slight 'revenge' for No 62 Squadron's losses at Lothar's hands the previous day. The ensuing dogfight cost No 62 Squadron two more Bristols, however — B1268 (2/Lt A. B. Well and Lt G. R. Crammond) and B1207 (2/Lt C. Allen and Lt N. T. Watson) — who apparently were victims of two pilots from Jagdstaffel 56 who had joined the fight. Afterwards the surviving F2B crews put in claims for a total of six enemy aircraft shot down: two of these were by the crew 2/Lt W. E. Staton and Lt H. E. Merritt in F2B C4619. 'Big Bill' Staton — as he was to become nicknamed in later years — ended his service with No 62 Squadron with a total of 26 victories (the unit's highest-scoring pilot) and eventually rose in RAF service to become Air Vice-Marshal CB, DSO, MC, DFC. Another tragic casualty for the squadron that day was F2B B1219, which crashed on a practice flight over the unit's airfield, killing Lt P. J. Batt and his Observer, 2/Lt F. J. McNiff. McNiff had only arrived to join the squadron some three hours before his death — his batman had not even unpacked the boy's belongings before the crash.

For No 20 Squadron February 1918 proved to be a successful month in terms of profit and loss. On 4 February a squadron OP tackled 20 Albatros scouts and rapidly disposed of nine of these, then rounded out the day by destroying a German kite balloon, with only one casualty, a wounded Observer. Next day four more victims fell to their guns, when the F2Bs engaged 12 Albatroses north of Staden just before noon; another two-seater was claimed on 16 February; while six German Albatros or Pfalz scouts were claimed by the late-morning OP on 17 February. Elsewhere the other F2B units were also taking a steady toll of German aircraft, with No 22 Squadron claiming 30 destroyed or out of control during the first three weeks of March 1918 without any losses to the squadron. On 15 March a patrol from No 62 Squadron met seven Albatroses over Esnes and drove four of these down, while the same unit claimed three more victims by 20 March.

Even as the pace of aerial activities quickened during February-March 1918, huge-scale plans and

Below:

F2B 'C' of No 22 Squadron at Vert Galand on 1 April 1918 — the day the RAF was born — with an Observer, Lt J. L. Morgan, in right foreground.

moves were being effected behind the German lines. With the collapse of the war in the east following Russia's 'October Revolution' in 1917 and its consequent release of vast numbers of men and quantities of war material for reinforcing the German armies in France et al, and equally significantly the Allied armies' bloodletting operations in France in late 1917, the German C-in-C, Ludendorff, steadily built up his ground and air forces for a massive land offensive in late March 1918. With the USA now a formally declared additional enemy of vast potential strength, Ludendorff wished to break the Allied armies quickly, before any American army came to the battle-lines, and accordingly instigated a priority air expansion programme during the winter of 1917-18, with special training of his airmen in support roles for an army offensive. Broadly, Ludendorff's aim was to drive a deep wedge between the main British and French armies south of Amiens and then 'roll up' the British BEF along the Channel coast. The essence of his offensive was to be surprise and speed initially, followed by massive reinforcement of advantages gained in rapid measure. On paper Ludendorff's plan looked both practical and unstoppable — but he had underestimated the value and importance of air power in opposition.

The distinct possibility of such a German spring offensive was by no means overlooked by the Allied army commanders and as early as 2 February Maj-Gen John Salmond — who had succeeded Hugh Trenchard in command of the RFC in France on 18 February 1918 — took measures to expand the British 5th Army's Bristol F2B unit, No 48 Squadron, by eight more aircraft in order to broaden aerial reconnaissance of the army's immediate front. By the end of February aerial photographs and other intelligence clearly indicated a most marked increase in German rail and road movements, apart from a further accumulation of dumps, light railways and aerodromes, while there appeared to be evidence that the German air service was not only being strengthened but also held back to a great extent from routine daily operations — most probably in preparation for an all-out offensive in the near future. RFC aerial reconnaissance was stepped up and continued to reveal the build-up of German strength — then for four days, from 17-20 March, thick clouds and rain made early morning recces impossible for the RFC. By then the specific duties of the RFC squadrons once any German offensive commenced had been defined and displayed, with maps, in the huts of every squadron. For their part in this scheme the Bristol F2B units were primarily to undertake low-level attacks on troops and transport, interspersed with strafing of German front-line troops. Specifically, No 48 Squadron was to reserve two of its Flights for such sorties, while the third Flight would continue to provide aerial recce patrols. By dawn of 21 March 1918 the Bristol F2B unit in France were located as follows:

Below:
Pilots and Observers of No 22 Squadron at Vert Galand, 1 April 1918. Of these, Lt R. Critchley (Observer, holding Lewis gun centre) and his pilot, Lt F. Williams (absent here), were shot down in flames the next day.
Imperial War Museum, Q11993

No 11 Squadron	Bellevue — OC, Maj R. F. S. Morton
No 20 Squadron	St Marie-Cappel — OC, Maj E. H. Johnston
No 22 Squadron	Serny — OC, Maj J. A. McKelvie
No 48 Squadron	Flez — OC, Maj H. S. Shield
No 62 Squadron	Cachy — OC, Maj F. W. Smith

In addition the following RFC squadrons had one or two F2Bs on strength:

Nos 10 (two), 12 (one), 15 (one) and 35 (two).

At 04.45hrs on 21 March some 6,500 German guns and 3,500 mortars commenced a unified barrage of pre-determined targets along the fronts held by the British 5th and 3rd Armies, between Arras and La Fere, raining high explosive and a proportion of gas shells of heavy calibre on to a thinly-stretched and surprised British front-line and reserve area. This hail of explosive came out of a densely misty sky which prevented any sizeable aerial activity by either British or German airmen, yet some RFC men made their initial efforts that day, engaging in ultra-low level ground-strafing of forward German infantry with machine guns and bombs and creating no little confusion among these spearhead troops; or as one German report described it, '. . . finding profitable targets in the thickly concentrated masses (of troops) . . .'. Such mud-height strafing onslaughts were to be the prime function of all RFC squadrons in the coming week, but as the initial German advance gained rapid depth into Allied-held territory, the weak British front-line forces were forced to give ground, while German artillery began shelling the various forward RFC airfields, and by dusk on 22 March no less than 17 RFC squadrons had been forced to evacuate their bases and fly to aerodromes farther back.

Space does not permit recording isolated individual efforts by the Bristol F2B crews from the many hundreds of similar sorties flown in the desperate weeks of March-April 1918. From first light until near-dark each day the RFC crews flew incessantly, pausing between sorties only to replenish ammunition belts, bomb racks and fuel tanks, with crews remaining beside their aircraft snatching a cup of tea and a bully beef sandwich — *if* available — and impatient to return to the fighting front. In the context of pure air combat the F2B crews between 21-31 March destroyed 36 enemy aircraft and claimed a further 17 as 'Out of control', for the losses of four F2Bs shot down in enemy territory and a further 13 men wounded in action or in flying accidents. Such victories were, nevertheless, secondary to their prime function — attacking the German infantry and transports. German army records for this period offered ample evidence of the daring and utter determination of all RFC aircrews involved in attempting to stem the German juggernaut advance, with accounts of infantry officers having to fling themselves flat on the ground to avoid actually being hit by low-flying RFC aircraft's undercarriages — indeed, even then one officer had an aircraft's wheels leave tyre-marks across his tunic back!

The first day of April 1918 dawned in fine weather, and shortly after 06.00hrs the first RAF patrols were taking-off for resumption of the unceasing offensive against the advancing German hordes who by then had gained 38 miles at their most forward point and captured some 1,200 square miles of former British-occupied territory. It was the day on which the new Royal Air Force was officially 'born', but the new labelling meant

Far left:
F2Bs of 'B' Flight, No 22 Squadron taking-off from Serny airfield on 17 June 1918. Pilots were (left to right) Capt W. F. J. Harvey and Lts H. H. Beddow, G. V. Wheatley and C. W. M. Thompson.

Left:
Extra muscle. A local modification of an additional Lewis gun for the pilot of F2B 'F' of No 22 Squadron (Sgt E. J. Elton DCM, MM). Note also the W/T generator on the lower port wing root.

nothing to the hard-pressed crews in France. Throughout the day the RAF crews claimed a total of 23 enemy aircraft and two observation balloons shot down: the only Bristol F2B claim was an Albatros DV shot down 'Out of control' by Lt C. L. Glover and Cpl W. Beales in C4701 of No 48 Squadron, although several other F2B crews had close combats in which several enemy aircraft were (at least) 'Driven down' with no visible positive results. Eight RAF aircraft and their crews were reported missing, but a further 14 were wrecked or 'lost' in faulty take-offs or landings — an overt indication of the tired states of many aircrews who by then were reaching physically and mentally exhausted states. Two Bristol F2Bs were among the aircraft lost to enemy action with C4615 of No 20 Squadron (Lts R. B. T. Hedges and A. G. Horlock) being hit by anti-aircraft fire in a mid-morning recce patrol and having their F2B set afire, though it was landed safely and its crew were unhurt; while another No 20 Squadron F2B, A7240 (Maj J. A. Dennistoun and Lt H. G. Crowe) also suffered a direct hit by AA fire and crash-landed at Wulverghem. Though the F2B was totally wrecked its crew returned to the squadron unhurt. Elsewhere the toll of aircraft returning with fuselages and wings tattered and bullet-riven finally required 28 aircraft being sent to Aircraft Repair Depots (ARDs) for refurbishment. Truly, the new air Service had been ushered into the world on a day in which its young aircrews had been well 'tested' in the crucible of savage and bloody conflict — yet in 'Bolo House' in central London that fateful day no less than 15 different 'committees' were sitting, solemnly debating the pros and cons of such matters as new badges of rank and a suitable uniform for the newly-born RAF.

By the first week in April 1918 the massive German offensive was visibly slowing to a halt, due principally to the stubborn resistance of some sections of the retreating British armies, but almost equally to the chaos and destruction of German supply transports and troop movements by the RAF crews over the previous weeks. Weather conditions continued to be unfavourable for flying, with dense mists and even snow on occasion, but the RAF crews did not slacken their pace of operations, continuing daily to harass and destroy German troop and transport movements. Then, on 9 April, Ludendorff set in motion his second offensive, this time farther north against the British 2nd Army in the Ypres-Armentieres zone, aiming to capture the Allied supply ports of Calais and Boulogne. Yet again the advancing German troops found themselves harried constantly by low-flying RAF aircraft and suffering heavy casualties from bombing and strafing onslaughts — losses which Ludendorff was to describe later as 'extraordinarily high' due to air action alone. With the focal point of the German advance aimed at Hazebrouck, this renewed battle raged on until the end of April, but to all intents began petering out slowly after 19 April. By then Ludendorff had already admitted privately that Germany could not win the war, and apart from one final outburst of heavy fighting on 24 April, the offensive on which Germany had pinned so much hope finally halted. A slight measure of the RFC/RAF's effort — and sacrifices — during the whole offensive may be obtained from the official statistics later recorded. Of the 1,232 first-line aircraft reported on squadron charge on 21 March 1918, 1,032 were written off charge — from *all* causes — within four weeks. Of these, 195 were reported as 'Missing', 696 as 'Wrecked' and a further 141 as burnt out or abandoned. In balance, RFC/RAF aircrews had claimed totals of 354

Right:
Fighting team. Capt W. E. Staton DSO, MC (holding propeller) and his usual Observer-gunner, Lt J. R. Gordon, of No 62 Squadron at Planque, in May 1918. Between them this pair were credited with 30 victories.

German aircraft destroyed and 188 'Out of control' — one of whom was the German 'Ace of aces', Rittmeister Manfred von Richthofen, who had been killed in action on 21 April.

In April two more F2B units supplemented the RAF strength in France, when No 59 Squadron, an RE8 unit at Vert Galand, commanded by Maj C. J. Mackay, began replacing its RE8s with F2Bs, completing re-equipment by September; then on 24 April a fresh F2B unit, No 88 Squadron, under the comand of Maj R. T. Leather, arrived from England to 'join the war', being based initially at Cappelle. Formed originally on 24 July 1917 at Gosport, No 88 Squadron was fully trained and equipped with Bristol F2Bs on arrival and therefore lost little time in commencing operations from 6 May; it claimed at least eight combat victories within its first two weeks of sorties. On the day following No 88 Squadron's debut, two crews from No 22 Squadron, 2/Lts A. C. Atkey and C. G. Gass, and 2/Lts J. E. Gurdon and A. J. Thornton, gave a remarkable demonstration of the fighting capabilities of well-handled Bristol Fighters, flying F2Bs B1164 and B1253 respectively. Setting out for an OP northeast of Arras, the two F2Bs first met a formation of seven Fokker D VIIs in the vicinity of Henin Lietard at some 15,000ft and immediately dived on these. This first attack saw each pilot shoot down a D VII apiece in flames, then as they pulled out of their dives each Observer in turn destroyed two more D VIIs as these attempted to get on the F2Bs' tails, both of these Germans also falling in flames. Even as this engagement was under way two more formations of D VIIs, some wearing green and white-painted tails, joined the fight, bringing the total enemy force up to about 20. Undeterred the F2B crews continued the fight for almost 30 minutes, during which time many D VIIs were seen spinning down, and when both Observers' guns had finally run out of ammunition, only seven D VIIs were still on the scene. By then four more D VIIs were confirmed as crashed — two by Atkey and one apiece having fallen to the guns of Gurdon and Gass. Both F2Bs then returned to base without further incident. Next day five No 22 Squadron crews claimed five enemy aircraft as destroyed, one crew being John Gurdon with Gass in his back cockpit. Not to be outdone, crews from No 20 Squadron claimed six enemy aircraft destroyed that same day, while other F2B units added two 'Out of control' to the day's tally.

By now Bristol Fighters were featuring prominently in the daily combat, taking a lion's share of credited aerial victories, and among the various squadrons no few F2B pilots and Observer-gunners were emerging as high-scoring individuals. Apart from Andrew McKeever of No 11 Squadron, another rising 'star-turn' — as RFC/RAF crews nicknamed their most outstanding pilots — was Capt Denis Latimer of No 20 Squadron, who was to be credited eventually with at least 29 victories and be awarded MC and DFC before 22 August 1918, when he was shot down in F2B D7993 to spend the rest of the war as a prisoner of the Germans. On 9 May four No 20 Squadron crews each claimed one German aircraft as destroyed, No 11 Squadron shot down nine (eight of these as 'Out of control'), and No 48 Squadron claimed three; but the day's biggest 'bag' was by No 22 Squadron which claimed 12 victories — five of these by the Atkey/Gass duo. Next day Capt G. F. Hughes MC, with Capt Hugh Claye as his gunner, shot down a German two-seater between Peronne and Combles as his 11th credited victory with No 62 Squadron, after which he returned to England and eventually pursued a flying career in his native Australia in postwar years.

Below:
E2514 'K' of No 22 Squadron (Lts S. M. Sellars and T. B. Collis), shot down on 27 August 1918 by Oberleutnant H. Frommherz, commander of Jasta 27.

Bottom:
E2529 which served with No 6 Squadron and, here, 'O' Flight of No 69 Squadron RFC (later retitled No 3 Squadron AFC).

It should be noted too that credited combat victories were not the prerogative of pilots, and many F2B Observer-gunners ran up relatively high 'scores' on their own account. Unlike the practice in certain other air services, gunners' victories were *not* automatically credited to their pilots — though it was a common joke among RFC/RAF aircrews that this was the way their 'drivers' gained medals and quick promotion! Among these 'back-seat aces' on the F2B units were such men as Lt L. A. Powell of No 11 Squadron (10 enemy aircraft) and Sgt J. J. Cowell (11), also of No 11 Squadron; Lt M. W. Waddington (11), Capt J. Hedley (12), Lt F. J. Ralph (five), Lt E. Hardcastle (six), Lt C. G. Boothroyd (nine), Lt H. L. Edwards (12½) and Lt T. C. Noel (10½) — all of No 20 Squadron; Sgt R. M. Fletcher (11), Lt C. G. Gass (16), Lt G. S. L. Hayward (eight), Sgt H. C. Hunt (seven) and Lt J. H. Umney (nine), of No 22 Squadron; Lts H. A. Cooper (five) and D. P. F. Uniacke (5½) of No 48 Squadron; Capt H. Claye (nine), Lts J. R. Gordon (five) and P. V. G. Chambers (seven) of No 62 Squadron. (The figure ½ equalled a share in a victory with another gunner or pilot.)

While the Bristol Fighter squadrons continued to regard German aircraft as their primary prey, the crews maintained daily routine photographic recce sorties, and in May No 20 Squadron particularly commenced unit bombing raids, carrying 112lb RL bombs, interspersed with its other duties. Employing the Bristol F2B as a day bomber was a negation of its design purpose since its structure was not specifically stressed for carriage of such items, and F2B crews carrying 112lb bombs under the aircraft fuselages soon realised how much the machine's performance was changed by such 'excrescences'. Normally, an F2B built up speed rapidly in any powered dive — with a 112lb 'between its legs' (sic) the diving speed increased appreciably and, in the graphic comment of one ex-No 20 Squadron pilot '. . . tended to give us premature grey hairs as the needle went right round the dial and stuck, while the Biff plunged down like a lead-lined brick'. Nevertheless, such raids remained a 'side show' to the more usual OPs, as on 14 May 1918 when one formation of six F2Bs dropped 112lb bombs on forward German troop concentrations, but a second patrol clashed with eight German scouts and quickly disposed of six of these. Next day No 20 Squadron contributed 24 112lb bombs to the total of 35 tons of bombs dropped by all RAF units by day, but the German airmen were out in some force throughout the day and the F2B units fought a number of fiercely-contested combats. No 11 Squadron's patrol fought high odds against a batch of 30 German scouts, losing one F2B (Capt J. V. Aspinall and Lt P. V. de la Cour), but claiming five enemy aircraft shot down; while No 22 Squadron claimed four Germans without loss; No 48 Squadron claimed two victims but lost two aircraft; No 62 Squadron shot down two without loss; and No 88 Squadron claimed one German scout crashed.

No 20 Squadron's daily bombing routine was maintained — delivering up to 35 112lb bombs in a single day on German rail centres et al — as was its combat record, with a particularly successful engagement on 19 May with 20 German scouts producing claims for seven enemy aircraft shot down. Other F2B squadrons claimed seven enemy aircraft shot down that day, but at a cost to No 62 Squadron of three aircraft down in enemy lines

Below:
E2260 of No 48 Squadron (Lts M. R. Mahony and J. R. Keir), brought down intact on 20 September 1918 by Lt Carl Degelow of Jasta 40 (fourth figure from left) for his 15th accredited victory. *A. E. Ferko*

(C796, C4630 and C4751), while a fourth, B1336 (Lts D. A. Savage MC and E. W. Collis) was attacked alone by nine German Albatroses and Pfalz scouts and shot down, landing near Corbie inside British lines. No 62 Squadron claimed revenge for these losses on 22 May when Capt W. E. Staton in F2B C874 led his patrol out of the sun to surprise a mixed gaggle of six German two-seaters and the F2Bs destroyed three of these. On 25 May a patrol from No 22 Squadron, led by Capt A. C. Atkey and Lt C. G. Gass, was escorting DH4 bombers from No 18 Squadron when a formation of some 40 German scouts attacked. The ensuing melee became so hotly contested that it was impossible to check whether the many enemy aircraft sent spinning out of the fight were 'Out of control' or merely manoeuvring for safety. In the event, once the sky cleared of hostile aircraft, four German scouts were seen crashed, while a fifth had been shot down in flames by Lt S. F. H. Thompson and Sgt R. M. Fletcher. Two days later another No 20 Squadron crew, Capt W. Beaver and Sgt E. Deighton, dived on nine enemy aircraft near Armentieres and destroyed one, then minutes later dived on a formation of Fokker triplanes. Deighton promptly despatched two of four triplanes which closed with the F2B, but when he ran out of ammunition his pilot shook off the remaining triplanes and returned to base, albeit in an aircraft liberally riddled with bullet holes and other damage. No 20 Squadron then closed its May 1918 'account' by shooting down eight enemy aircraft during the course of a patrol on 31 May, while No 22 Squadron claimed three, and No 88 Squadron one, on the same day; though No 62 Squadron lost one F2B reported 'Missing', but its crew returned to base.

June 1 provided a minor heat-wave in weather and activity was brisk throughout the day for the F2B squadrons. Lt W. M. Thomson and 2/Lt G. H. Kemp in C843 of No 20 Squadron were cut off from the other eight F2Bs of their patrol by four enemy scouts. Turning into these Thomson destroyed one with 200 rounds at 50yd range, then his gunner, Kemp, firing at a second from 25yd range and sent it down to crash. At that moment an Albatros dived and killed Kemp with its first burst, but by spinning down Thomson was eventually able to shake off further attacks. Meanwhile the remainder of his patrol were busy fighting a force of 25 Pfalz and Albatroses, with the crews of C892 (Capt D. Latimer and T. C. Noel) and C4764 (Lts V. E. Groom and E. Hardcastle) shooting down three Germans to crash. Groom remained in the RAF after the war and eventually retired as Air Marshal Sir Victor Groom KCVO, KBE, CB, DFC. For No 20 Squadron these were the first of 35 combat victories claimed by the unit's crews throughout June 1918, many of these by several of 20's most successful F2B pilots and gunners who included four Americans (Lts C. Oberst and the brothers August and Paul Iaccaci, and Lt E. W. Sweeny, USAS), as well as such high-scoring pilots as Capt T. P. Middleton MC, DFC, Capt F. Godfrey DFC, Lts W. M. Thomson, L. H. T. Capel and D. J. Weston, and equally successful Observer-gunners like Hardcastle, Deighton and Sgt A. Newlands. Another No 20 Squadron 'ace', Capt H. P. Lale, joined the unit in late June, having already seen fighting service with No 48 Squadron, and eventually was credited with a war tally of 20 victories.

Below:
Five long-range reconnnaissance Flights, lettered L, M, N, O and P, were specially formed in 1918 equipped with F2Bs. This example was F5812 (a rebuilt aircraft) serving with 'L' Flight, with (from left) AM Dixon, Capt B. E. Catchpole MC, DFC (OC Flight), and 2/Lt A. J. Findley.

Below:
Seen in 1918 is B1134 '19' of No 35 Squadron, which had previously served with No 48 Squadron. *G. Stuart Leslie*

Bottom:
C4692 '43', of No 4 Auxiliary School of Aerial Gunnery, Marske, with a camera gun fitted above the upper wing centre-section.
G. Stuart Leslie

Relatively speaking, June 1918 proved to be a reasonably quiet month for the Bristol F2B squadrons, though by no means devoid of combats, casualties or operational flights on various duties. One unforeseen cause of the overall lessening of aerial activity was an epidemic of so-termed 'Spanish influenza' which spread across Europe, the effects of which incapacitated many airmen in France; indeed, at one stage in the following month of July No 62 Squadron alone had up to 20 pilots or Observers hors de combat with the virus, and most units suffered similar 'casualties' in varying degrees, thereby reducing the number of available fit crews for daily operations. By the end of June 1918, however, Bristol F2B crews in France had claimed an overall total of 60 enemy aircraft brought down throughout the month, but had suffered the losses of 11 F2Bs to direct combat action, 24 crewmen known killed or reported 'Missing', and a further 12 men wounded in combat or injured in flying accidents. For much of the month No 20 Squadron had mounted a series of bombing raids, in particular against the German-occupied town of Armentieres, but usually flew at least three separate patrols each day with at least two of these being straightforward OPs seeking the German air service in the skies. While combats were a frequent feature of such patrols, large formations of German fighters were rarely met, with at least one notable exception on 30 June. In the early evening

Left:
Of several Home Defence units to use F2Bs in 1917-18, No 39 Squadron began re-equipment in November 1917. This example, B1330, '2', had seen previous service with Nos 11 and 22 Squadrons, and was a presentation aircraft named *Darbangha No 5*.

Below left:
Only two Home Defence F2Bs scored confirmed aerial victories over England. This F2B, C4636 (Lt A. J. Arkell and AM A. T. C. Stagg) of No 39 Squadron, shot down a Gotha raider on the night of 19/20 May 1918.

14 F2Bs set out on a hunt for Germans and at 19.30hrs ran into a total of 16 Fokker D VIIs and Pfalz scouts, with a single all-black Fokker triplane, over Comines-Wervicq. The Germans were in two layers of nine and seven aircraft and the nine higher Germans became the first targets for the F2Bs who engaged these at some 10,000ft. F2B C951 (Capt T. P. Middleton and Capt F. Godfrey), leading the OP, dived on the all-black triplane and both men fired into it in turn. The 'Tripehound' (the most common RAF nickname for the Fokker Dr1 triplane) fell away and eventually crashed east of Comines. Minutes later the F2Bs dived on a batch of eight Pfalz and eventually destroyed six of these in crashes with two others claimed as 'Out of control', One F2B, C938 (Lt T. C. Traill and 2/Lt E. Hardcastle), had a particularly hectic 20 minutes during this latter fight, diving on various enemy aircraft until eventually finding themselves at only 2,000ft north of Comines with Traill's front gun jammed. As he cleared the jam, several Germans bore in and liberally riddled the F2B, creating serious damage, but the crew fought them off and sent one down out of control before Hardcastle's Lewis gun also jammed. By then the damage to the F2B had left Traill with only minimal control but he managed to force-land in a field northwest of St Omer, only to collide with a French cow and kill it, apart from doing further damage to his Bristol Fighter. Traill was yet another F2B pilot who remained in the RAF as his career, eventually retiring as Air Vice-Marshal CB, OBE, DFC.

By early 1918 no few F2B Observer-gunners had begun fitting twin yoked Lewis guns on their Scarff Ring mountings to double their fire-power for offence/defence, and of necessity stowing more drums of ammunition in their cockpits; this reflection of their offensive spirit was matched equally by certain pilots attempting to mount one or even two extra Lewis guns on locally-made mountings above the upper wing, firing over the propeller arc. The overall weight penalties of such additional warloads on the F2B's performance were surprisingly small and accepted by crews in view of the greater opportunities for 'hitting the Hun harder' (sic). Nevertheless, when the F2Bs were detailed for bombing raids, especially when loaded with 112lb RL bombs, crews usually reverted to the standard two guns arrangement — there were, after all, limits to the doughty Bristol Fighter's 'patience'. . . . Normal ammunition loads for the standard forward Vickers and rear Lewis were up to 1,200 rounds for the Vickers and seven drums (97 rounds each) for the Lewis, including the drum mounted on the gun prior to take-off and six stowed drums around the rear cockpit interior.

July 1918 opened with some brisk clashes with German scouts. On 2 July nine F2Bs of No 20 Squadron were on an OP when they clashed with fighters from Jagdstaffel 56's Pfalz and Fokker D VIIs. In the fight the F2B crews claimed at least three Germans as destroyed but lost two aircraft — D8090 (Lt H. C. McCreary and Sgt W. J. H. Barter) and C850 (Lt P. T. Davidson and Sgt J. Helsby) — both in flames. (Since Jasta 56's records show no casualties on this date, these German aircraft were probably from another unit which joined the fight as it progressed. Any dogfight usually attracted any other fighters — RAF or German — in the vicinity.) Lt T. C. Traill and 2/Lt P. G. Jones in B1344 were surprised by one Fokker D VII whose fire killed Jones and shot away the F2B's aileron controls, forcing Traill to land at St Marie Cappel. On the same date No 48

Squadron claimed three victories without loss to the F2Bs. Six days later Capt Bill Staton led six F2Bs from No 62 Squadron on a joint OP with Sopwith Camels of No 73 Squadron and dived on six Fokker triplanes near Lille. Between them the F2Bs and Camels shot down three triplanes (two to No 62 Squadron) but lost F2B C1002 (Lt J. A. Chubb and Sgt J. Borwein) who fell victim to Leutnant Paul Billik of Jagdstaffel 52. For No 22 Squadron the first big engagement of the month came on 10 July, when nine F2Bs from this unit ran into a mixed formation of 15-20 Fokker triplanes and Pfalz scouts. Lt John Gurdon and J. J. Scaramanga dived on one Pfalz and sent it down pouring flames but were then attacked by two other Germans whose fire severely wounded Scaramanga in his rear cockpit. Despite his wounds Scaramanga fought back and shot both of his adversaries down out of control. In all eight, possibly 10, German scouts were brought down, though No 22 Squadron lost one Bristol (Lts H. M. Dickinson and M. H. Kane MC) and had two Observers badly wounded; Scaramanga only lived for a few minutes after landing back at base. Elsewhere that day No 48 Squadron suffered the loss of an F2B piloted by the American Lt E. D. Shaw USAS and his Observer, Sgt T. Smith.

The remainder of the month passed with relatively routine activities, but with the 'balance' of casualties in favour of the enemy airmen. F2B squadrons throughout the month lost 13 aircraft in combat, 34 men killed or 'Missing', and a further 12 wounded or injured, and only claimed 49 combat victories, mostly in the doubtful category of 'Out of control'. On 19 July No 88 Squadron was transferred from the aegis of the 65th Wing to the 80th Wing and accordingly moved its base from Cappelle to Drionville, while on 30 July No 22 Squadron also moved base, from Serny to Maisoncelle. These moves were matched by several other RAF units at this period as one small part of general Allied preparations for an imminent land offensive. The focal point of this projected offensive was east of Amiens, along an 11 miles' frontage just south of the Amiens-Roye road to Morlancourt, and the F2B units (along with other squadrons) were briefed to despatch aircraft in pairs at half-hour intervals from zero-hour-plus-20 minutes from the first day. This offensive, commonly titled the Battle of Amiens, commenced on 8 August, but fog shrouding the battle area prevented aerial activity for several hours after zero hour. Then as the fog began to lift the RAF crews were out on their low-level sorties, strafing and bombing German rear areas as the Allied armies advanced rapidly through the clinging mists and took forward German trenches and gun batteries completely by surprise. On the day before, No 62 Squadron had moved its base from Planques to Croisette, near St Pol, and then began a series of escort sorties protecting day bomber raids interspersed with OPs; it claimed two enemy aircraft shot down on 8 August, three more on 10 August and five more on 12 August, but at a cost of the loss of F2B E2468 (2/Lt J. N. Mitchell and Lt A. B. Cort) on 12 August. On 11 August No 20 Squadron despatched 16 F2Bs each carrying 112lb bombs to raid Courtrai, with three SE5A fighter squadrons as escort, a mini-armada of some 40 aircraft in all. The F2Bs bombed their target without interference, then flew back at low level and strafed German observation balloons en route, sending four of these down burning.

No 48 Squadron's F2B crews claimed one enemy aircraft shot down on 8 August but lost two F2Bs and an Observer wounded, while No 88 Squadron claimed two victories for a cost of two men wounded; the 'balance' of successes was to some extent restored when at 09.25hrs No 22 Squadron sent up its total available strength of 15 F2Bs to escort DH4s from No 18 Squadron on a raid against Somain rail junction. Ten German scouts attempted to attack the bombers but were quickly dispersed by 22's crews who claimed five as shot down. Two days later two F2B crews from the same squadron attacked 12 Fokker D VIIs and destroyed four of them. On 11 August No 88 Squadron tackled a formation of about 25 Fokker D VIIs and in a fierce fight claimed five of these, apart from a sixth enemy aircraft destroyed on a later patrol that day. The pace of combat heightened steadily over the next few days, with No 22 Squadron claiming nine victories during a single bomber-escort sortie on 13 August, to add to three other claims by other F2B units on that date — all without F2B losses. Four more victories were claimed on 14 August, but this time two F2Bs failed to return — one each from Nos 20 and 88 Squadrons. On 16 August came an innovation in RAF tactics when four squadrons of the 80th Wing — Nos 88 (F2B), 92 (SE5A), 2 AFC (SE5A) and 4 AFC (Camels) — combined for a Wing raid on Haubourdin aerodrome: a total of 65 aircraft in unit 'layers' from 13,000ft down to 7,000ft, led overall by Lt-Col Louis Strange DSO, MC. The F2Bs' role was as top aerial cover and the raid proved highly successful with no RAF losses. Next day the same four squadrons, again led by Strange, repeated the tactic by bombing and strafing Lomme aerodrome, although this time stiff ground-fire claimed one of No 4 AFC's Camels.

August 24 became the blackest day in the annals of No 48 Squadron. Despite the official communique's comment that 'Enemy aircraft activity was slight', 48's aerodrome at Bertangles was attacked by German bombers during the evening and bombs scored direct hits on five hangars, destroying nine F2Bs and damaging two others, apart from wrecking most of the unit's heavy transport and other equipment. The most serious casualties however were among some 200 men packed inside one hangar attending an entertainment concert. Of these, No 48 Squadron suffered two aircrewmen killed and 14 others badly wounded by bomb splinters, apart from four others slightly injured. Next morning the unit commander, Maj Keith Park MC, found that only five F2Bs remained flyable, and on 26 August he led these to a new base at Boisdinghem, where new F2Bs and replacements of flying crews were very quickly provided to bring the squadron to full fighting strength again. (Two of the German bombers, a Gotha GVb and a Friedrichshafen, were shot down by two Camel pilots from No 151 Squadron.) On the same day (26 August) No 20 Squadron vacated Boisdinghem to move to Vignacourt. By the end of the month No 22 Squadron had four more crews killed or 'Missing', while the monthly statistics for August 1918 showed that 47 enemy aircraft had been claimed by F2B crews, as against 10 F2Bs shot down, 26 crewmen killed or 'Missing', and 28 others 'Wounded'.

Though the August figures for casualties were grim enough, they were merely preliminaries to much higher losses (and victory claims) in September, which month proved to be the most intense of the year in the context of F2B aerial combat. The first six days' fighting in September cost the F2B squadrons nine aircraft shot down, two other crewmen killed, and eight more wounded. On 15 September, for one example, Bristol crews claimed nine enemy aircraft destroyed but lost three F2Bs and had an Observer wounded. Next day No 20 Squadron again moved its base, this time to Suzanne, but the move did not interrupt patrols and in the course of that day its crews claimed three enemy aircraft brought down; while other F2B squadrons claimed five victories but also lost five aircraft and crews and had two other men wounded. A particularly outstanding example of cool determination that day was demonstrated by No 11 Squadron crew, Capt E. S. Coler and 2/Lt E. J. Corbett, who were attacked by a large number of German scouts whose fire holed one of the F2B's petrol tanks and shot away its aileron controls. Diving to 1,000ft above Cambrai, the F2B was again attacked by two Germans who overshot their prey. Turning on to the tail of one of his tormentors, Coler shot it down in flames, while Corbett put paid to its companion. Crossing the lines at barely 150ft, Coler felt the F2B becoming uncontrollable and therefore, with calm skill, slowly side-slipped the aircraft down to a crash-landing without injury to himself or his observer.

On 20 September a fresh crew to No 48 Squadron, Lt M. R. Mahoney and 2/Lt J. N. Keir, set out on their first operational sortie, flying F2B E2260, as the tail-ender of a 'Vic' of three F2Bs. At about the same time Leutnant Carl Degelow of Jagdstaffel 40 took off from Halluin, north of Lille, on a pre-breakfast air test of his recently overhauled Fokker D VII. On reaching 9,000ft Degelow spotted the trio of F2Bs and cautiously closed on the tail of the rearmost, E2260, which was straggling behind its companions. Pouncing out of the sun, Degelow fired and was immediately met with return fire from the alert gunner, Keir. The F2B then dived away in a lengthy flat glide and after a few more brief exchanges of fire between Keir and Degelow, the rear Lewis gun jammed solid. Realising this Degelow withheld further

Below:

Crews of No 141 (HD) Squadron at Biggin Hill in 1918, with Maj B. E. Baker (OC) standing seventh from right. A No 141 Squadron F2B, C851 (Lts E. E. Turner and H. B. Barwise), shot down Gotha GV No 979/16 of *Bogohl 3* on the night of 19/20 May 1918.

firing and shepherded the now helpless Bristol down to a landing near Roubaix — his 21st *luftsieg*, intact, and with a live crew to boot! Later that day a patrol from No 20 Squadron, reinforced by some SE5As from No 84 Squadron, engaged 20 Fokkers over St Quentin, and in the unusually lengthy (30 minutes) dogfight which followed claimed at least six Fokkers for a cost of two crewmen killed. On 23 September No 20 Squadron claimed four more victories but lost an F2B and had one gunner wounded, then next day was on the move yet again, shifting base to Proyart. From here, on 25 September, the unit put up a patrol of nine F2Bs in the early evening which clashed with some 15-20 Fokkers northeast of St Quentin and proceeded to shoot down seven Germans to crashes with an eighth 'Out of control', three of the confirmed destroyed falling to the guns of Capt G. H. Hooper and 2/Lt H. Edwards in F2B E2536. Two days later F2B squadrons claimed six victories but lost seven F2Bs throughout the day, while on that day No 62 Squadron moved from Croisette to Bellevue airfield. September 29 brought four more claims for victories by F2B crews, offset by the losses of four F2Bs and their crews, and on the following day No 48 Squadron left Boisdinghem, now fully up to strength, and moved to St Marie Cappel. September 1918 had been a fateful month for F2B squadrons. For a total of 95 enemy aircraft claimed as brought down, they had lost totals of 33 aircraft shot down in combat, 76 crewmen killed or 'Missing', and a further 21 men wounded — virtually the full establishment in crews and machines of three complete F2B squadrons.

By the beginning of October 1918 the rapid advances of the Allied armies had forced the opposing German armies into a steady retreat which gained momentum as the month progressed. All RAF squadrons now concentrated upon bombing and low-level strafing sorties against the retreating German troops, but aerial combat continued to the very end, with the German staffeln offering a fierce resistance despite diminishing facilities for maintenance and lack of fuel, ammunition and other necessities. The F2B units, as with most other RAF squadrons, were kept constantly moving forward to maintain contact with their advancing armies as these travelled eastwards, often occupying fresh quarters for merely a few days before flying on to new airfields evacuated by German units. Throughout October the F2B squadrons claimed a total of 43 enemy aircraft shot down, but at a cost of seven F2Bs, 22 men killed or 'Missing', and 13 wounded. By November diplomatic overtures for an armistice by the German authorities were already in motion, and operations gradually declined during the early days of the month. For most RAF units 10 November proved to be their ultimate day for war sorties. On that date No 20 Squadron despatched a patrol of seven F2Bs just before noon to seek out German aircraft, and these spotted seven German scouts attacking a formation of DH9 bombers in the vicinity of Charleroi. Diving to the bombers' rescue, the F2Bs sent down four Germans to crash and a fifth was claimed as 'Out of control'. Two F2Bs were lost, however, when F4421 and F6195 were shot down with three of their four crewmen being killed.

Next morning, at the eleventh hour of the eleventh day of the eleventh month of 1918, an armistice officially came into force and all hostilities legally ceased. Those first days of November had cost the F2B squadrons five aircraft and their crews lost in combat, though 11 German aircraft had been claimed as shot down. Despite the official declaration of 'peace', all RAF units remained at full war-readiness for several weeks, prepared to quell any renewed outbreak of hostilities by dissident German groups, but aerial activity was mainly comprised of reconnaissance patrols over the masses of disillusioned and disorganised former enemy armies as these made their way by any available means back to their utterly defeated homelands. As one veteran F2B pilot described his feelings during those first few weeks of peace:

'Flying low over hordes of field-grey uniformed troops, all heading eastwards, brought home to me the completeness of Germany's defeat. Rarely did any German even bother to look up at our aircraft, but kept their heads bowed as they trudged wearily homewards. It seemed so unreal, I found myself automatically twisting my neck at regular intervals, scanning the sky above for German fighters about to attack, watching any cloud which might conceal a host of Fokkers. Old habits die hard, especially self-preservation, and it was many days before my brain accepted the simple fact that there were no more marauding Fokkers up there waiting to pounce. Then came another strange reaction — I found myself being ultra-cautious about my flying, watching very carefully that I didn't make some stupid error in judgment. I suppose it was the sight of several fellows on nearby squadrons killing themselves doing unnecessary aerobatics; having survived eight months of flying in France I was going to make bloody sure I got home in one piece . . . ! Most of my squadron's pilots made something of a ceremony of having 'one last flip' in their Bristols the day before they left for HE (Home Establishment, ie, to England), but when my orders for posting to England arrived I merely had my Flight Sergeant remove the F2B's serial number from its fin and put this in my bag; I wasn't going to tempt Fate one jot more . . . !

Above the Deserts

With the formal declaration of war on Turkey by Britain and France on 5 November 1914, the necessity for defence of the vital Suez Canal link on the line of communications of the British Empire led to an immediate detachment of the Royal Flying Corps to Egypt for defence of that waterway. Comprising three officers and 37 non-commissioned personnel, this detachment arrived in Alexandria on 17 November 1914 and became based at Ismailia, equipped with three Maurice Farman aircraft brought from England, two Henry Farmans obtained from Heliopolis, and two Maurice Farmans and a BE2a (all without engines) received from India. In addition seven French seaplanes were put at the disposal of the British C-in-C, Egypt. From these humble beginnings the RFC, and later RAF, presence in the various countries bordering the eastern Mediterranean was to enlarge and extend its influence steadily over the following four years of war, and indeed many decades thereafter.

The arrival of the Bristol F2B above the deserts came with the initial formation of No 111 Squadron RFC on 1 August 1917, when a Flight of No 14 Squadron RFC, based at Deir El Belah in Palestine, was detached from its parent to become the nucleus of the new squadron. Commanded by Maj A. Shekleton, No 111 Squadron commenced war flights on 10 August, and by the end of September 1917 had its full establishment of three Flights, equipped overall with one Bristol Scout, two Bristol M1 monoplane scouts, four de Havilland scouts, five Vickers FB19 scouts, and six Bristol F2B Fighters. On 5 October, along with No 67 Squadron, the new unit formed 40th Army Wing under the command of Lt-Col A. E. 'Biffy' Borton DSO, under the aegis of the Palestine Brigade. The Bristol F2Bs of No 111 Squadron were soon in action, and on 8 October 1917 one F2B crewed by Lt R. C. Steele and Lt J. J. Lloyd-

Below:
F2B A7194, which served with No 111 Squadron RFC and No 1 Squadron AFC in Palestine. *K. Johanesson*

Right:
Maj S. W. Addison (left) and Lt W. Hudson Fysh (later, Sir Hudson) DFC in front of F2B A7200 of No 1 Squadron AFC, Palestine, in 1918 — an aircraft nicknamed 'The Yellow Peril'.

Williams intercepted two Albatros scouts and shot one down in Allied lines. The German pilot was unwounded and his Albatros little damaged, so the squadron's mechanics quickly refurbished it to flying status again. On 15 October the same F2B crew intercepted three Albatros scouts as these crossed over into Allied territory. In his first attack Steele put one Albatros's engine out of action, and its pilot hand-signalled his apparent intention to land and began gliding down. Steele naturally withheld further fire and followed the German down, only to realise that the German was deliberately gliding towards the Turkish lines. Steele signalled to the Albatros pilot to turn back, but when this signal was ignored Steel's Observer re-opened fire and shot off one of the Albatros's wings. Steele, a Canadian, was later awarded a DSO, while Lloyd-Williams received an MC.

By the end of October 1917 the squadron had begun receiving SE5As, and by January 1918 Nieuport Scouts, to replace its somewhat mixed bag of aircraft types, with the ultimate intention of becoming a single-seat scout unit. The changeover was, however, a slow process, but in the interim No 111 Squadron's F2Bs continued operations. On 12 December, for example, one of its Flight commanders, Capt R. M. Drummond, with an air mechanic as his gunner, was escorting two two-seaters from No 67 (Australian) Squadron RFC on a recce patrol when three Albatros scouts appeared over Tul Keram and were obviously preparing to attack. Drummond immediately set off to tackle this trio alone. His first victim spun down and crashed, and Drummond then chased after its two companions. An accurate burst into one caused it to break up in mid-air, while the remaining Albatros, flying very low and apparently trying to land in a hurry, flew into the side of a hill. Drummond was later to rise in RAF service to become Air Marshal Sir Peter R. M. Drummond KCB, DSO, OBE, MC. As SE5As and Nieuport scouts arrived for No 111 Squadron its Bristol F2Bs were transferred piecemeal to No 67 (Australian) Squadron, machine for machine, to replace the Australians' RE8s, BE2Cs and Martinsyde G102s. Thus by the end of January 1918 the Australian unit had a strength of nine F2Bs, two RE8s, five Martinsydes and five BEs, with the 'one-for-one' exchange still continuing. On 6 February No 67 (Australian) Squadron RFC became officially retitled as No 1 Squadron, Australian Flying Corps (AFC), and by the end of the same month No 111 Squadron had struck off unit charge its last F2B, while by the end of March 1918 No 1 Squadron AFC was up to full establishment of 18 Bristol F2Bs.

No 1 Squadron AFC had originally left its native homeland as a complete unit (and with that title) on 16 March 1916, and disembarked in Egypt where it became based at Heliopolis for defence of the Suez Canal. Here it was retitled No 67 (Australian) Squadron RFC on 12 September 1916, and by the close of 1917 — after continuous and splendid operational service in support of British and Australian forces battling against the Turks — was based in Palestine. Until then its air and ground crews had fought manfully with outmoded BE and Martinsyde aircraft, supplemented by equally vulnerable RE8s, so the advent of the greatly superior F2B was welcomed enthusiastically by the offensive-minded Australians, and they were quick to exploit the F2B's prowess. Initially the F2Bs were used primarily for long-range reconnaissance and/or fighting escorts to recce aircraft, but on 3 January 1918 a combined formation of 16 RFC aircraft — eight from No 67 Squadron — attacked the enemy at El Afule, delivering some 1,200lb of high explosive bombs on target. On their return flight the formation was attacked by two Albatros scouts. One of the escort F2Bs, B1128, crewed by Lts R. A. Austin and L. W. Sutherland, climbed above the Albatroses,

Below:
A7192 of No 1 Squadron AFC.

Bottom:
Ramleh aerodrome, Palestine, base for No 111 Squadron RAF and No 1 Squadron AFC.

attacked one, and shot it down to crash — the first officially confirmed combat victory for the unit's F2Bs. The other Albatros tried to attack one of the RE8s but was sent spinning down out of control by the RE's gunner. On 17 January two F2Bs were on a recce patrol south of Nablus at 11,000ft when two separate formations of enemy scouts appeared — five Albatroses 500ft below and three others about 1,000ft above them — yet these appeared reluctant to attack the pair of F2Bs. One F2B (Lts L. M. Potts and F. Hancock) dived on the lower Albatroses and fired 30 rounds into the rearmost scout which immediately flipped over on to its back, then fell away apparently out of control. The remaining Albatroses made a few half-hearted passes but then left the area — an indication of their respect for the Bristol F2B, which was to become even more evident in the following months.

Meanwhile Gen Allenby's forces had captured Jerusalem on 9 December 1917, but the city was still within range of Turkish guns, and in order to ensure the security of Jerusalem and Jaffa, Allenby decided to mount a further offensive aimed at Jericho with the intention of driving the Turks back across the River Jordan, and this advance was planned to commence on 19 February 1918. In the weeks preceding this attack all RFC units became busy photographing the Turkish lines and reserve areas; No 1 Squadron AFC photographing 624 square miles of enemy territory

during the last two weeks in January alone. In between such recces the Australians undertook several bombing raids against railway junctions and Turkish gun emplacements. The Jericho offensive was duly launched on time and on 21 February British cavalry were entering the city, now devoid of all Turkish occupation. While this successful attack secured the right flank of Allenby's armies, it became merely a preliminary to further offensives in the coming months. Air

activity continued at an intense pace, with the Australian F2Bs penetrating deeply over Turkish areas. On 9 March the squadron joined with the recently formed No 142 Squadron in attacks on Turkish positions on the Lubban-Nablus road, dropping 150 bombs and creating serious damage and casualties.

Enemy aircraft were only occasionally met during these operations, but on each such occasion the F2Bs immediately engaged, as on 5 March when two F2Bs — Lts Headlam and E. B. S. Beaton, and Lts C. N. Watt and T. C. Macaulay — were jumped by five Albatros scouts. The F2Bs shot two down out of control and dispersed the others. On 21 March Allenby's troops began a projected advance across the River Jordan to Amman, but this attack petered out and by 2 April all Allied forces had withdrawn to their former positions. During these operations the RFC squadrons had done their utmost in support, including an innovation (for this theatre) whereby aircraft picked up messages from the ground forces by trailing below the fuselages a line with weighted hook which snatched written instructions suspended in the middle of a cord stretched between two poles — a form of 'army co-operation' used extensively by Bristol F2B squadrons of the RAF during the 1920s. Further attempted Allied advances in late April/early May were also frustrated by strong Turkish opposition; these were failures exacerbated by the vital need for more troops in France to stem the German spring offensive which led to many of Allenby's most experienced divisions being transferred to France and being replaced by inexperienced Indian infantry and cavalry in Palestine and Mesopotamia. Thus during April and May 1918 No 1 Squadron AFC became primarily a recce unit, flying daily east of the Jordan and Dead Sea. These patrols began meeting increased opposition from enemy airmen and several clashes were reported. On 3 June Lts P. J. McGuinness and Hudson Fysh in F2B A7237 met a particularly tough Rumpler two-seater near Jericho and exhausted all their ammunition upon it without visible result before breaking off the fight.

The enemy's respect for the Bristol F2Bs of the Australian squadron was amply evidenced in a captured diary, where an entry dated 4 April 1918 said: 'The enemy, who possesses in his Bristol Fighter an exceptionally fine machine, has made himself lately very redoubtable. Nearly always flying in twos, the Bristol Fighters present an extraordinary fighting force, and their harassing of our activities becomes more and more felt.' Yet it should be remarked that the Bristol F2B alone was not the key to the RAF's successes in this theatre of war. The German squadrons had Albatros D Va scouts, later supplemented by Pfalz scouts, and equally fast and efficient two-seater aircraft such as Rumpler CVs, AEGs and the latest LVGs. The difference in achievements lay truly with the airmen concerned flying these aircraft. Whereas the German airmen, brave and technically as skilled as most RAF crews, tended to fight to rigidly laid-down tactics, the Australian crews

Left:
Trophy. Albatros D.III No 636/17 was shot down on 8 October 1917 by Lt R. C. Steele of No 111 Squadron RFC. Its pilot, Obltn Hägelstern, became a prisoner of war.

Right:
Capt D. W. Rutherford with F2B B1146 of No 1 Squadron AFC at El Mejdel, Palestine in April 1918. Note the presentation inscription.
Via R. Vann

Below:
Hardware. Lt Fred Haig of No 1 Squadron AFC with examples of armament used, including 112lb RL/20lb Hale/16lb HE/100lb Hale bombs, plus stripped Lewis and a Vickers machine gun mounted for airfield defence.

mixed a constant offensive-minded outlook with daring and flexibility in tactics, flying their F2Bs to known limits — and often beyond. During April and May clashes with German scouts usually meant the F2Bs tackling numerically superior odds, yet every such clash resulted in victory — either material or moral — for the Bristol crews. F2B casualties mostly occurred from other causes than enemy aircraft, as on 1 May when two F2Bs — Lts D. W. Rutherford and J. McElligott and Lts F. Haig and R. T. Challinor — set off on a dawn recce, and to drop leaflets to the Beni Sakr Arabs. Near Amman machine gun fire from the ground ruptured both petrol tanks in Rutherford's F2B and he force-landed, burning his machine. Haig immediately landed alongside the burning wreckage and took Rutherford and McElligott aboard, but on taking off one wheel collapsed, tipping the F2B on its nose. Setting fire to Haig's machine, all four men then surrendered to some Circassian cavalry which arrived on the scene shortly after.

Fights with enemy aircraft during May brought more victories for the F2B crews. On 22 May Capt Ross Smith and Lt W. A. Kirk, and Lts E. P. Kenny and W. J. A. Weir, fought two Albatros scouts at 11,000ft over Nablus. Attacking these from below, the F2B gunners only fired and both Albatroses fell away, obviously out of control, without any return fire. At about the same time a pair of F2Bs — Lts C. S. Paul and Weir, and Lts A. V. Tonkin and R. A. Camm — patrolling south of Nablus met four Albatroses and attacked these at 12,000ft near Huwara. Both pilots shot

down an Albatros each on their first attack, then Paul and Weir had a running scrap with a third Albatros which continued until both aircraft were near the ground near Nablus. Making one final dive, Paul overflew his opponent but then saw the Albatros force-land and heavily flip over on to its back. Waiting until its pilot had crawled out of the wreck, the F2B crew then chased him to cover with crisp bursts of 'near-misses'. Just seven days later two other F2Bs — Lts E. C. Stooke and Weir and Lts G. C. Peters and J. H. Traill — cornered a two-seater near the same spot and sent it down in flames. On 4 June, however, two of No 1 Squadron's rare air combat casualties occurred when Lts Tonkin and Camm approached a Rumpler over Jerusalem from out of the sun and manoeuvred underneath it before the German two-man crew were aware of the F2B's presence. Elevating his twin Lewis guns, Camm opened fire only to have his right-hand gun jam. Tonkin then attempted to use his forward Vickers but this jammed too. By then the Rumpler's gunner had retaliated, putting a burst into the F2B's engine which sprayed water over Tonkin. As Tonkin turned away the Rumpler's gunner fired one more burst and wounded Camm in his wrist, and therefore Tonkin landed at the nearest field hospital, Camm's wound being serious enough to cause him to be invalided back to Australia. On 27 June another casualty from groundfire was F2B A7236 which crashed in the hills of Lebanon after its pilot, Lt G. V. Oxenham, was fatally wounded, though its Observer, Lt L. H. Smith, survived as a prisoner of war. Oxenham's loss was avenged next day when two F2Bs attacked six Albatroses near Amman and succeeded in shooting down at least two.

For much of June and early July 1918 the F2Bs indulged themselves by a series of ground-strafing sorties, attacking troops, transports, camel trains and even enemy airfields, a form of offensive much to the crews' liking. By mid-July the enemy airmen began appearing more frequently of late, but were always immediately engaged and — almost always — throughly routed. On 17 July Capt Ross Smith and Lt Lirk destroyed two Albatros scouts over Wadi el Auja; on the 22nd Lts Tonkin and McCann destroyed a Rumpler; on 24 July Lts Peters and Traill and Walker and Letch shot down a two-seater north of Mejdel Yaba; on the 28th a particularly brave Rumpler crew fought two F2Bs before being forced to land and then killed by the F2Bs' strafing fire; while on the 30th another Rumpler went down under the guns of Lts Kenny and Sutherland. On 2 August two F2Bs tackled four German two-seaters, destroyed one and sent two others down out of control; then on 14 August the Bristol crews had their first encounter with newly-arrived German Pfalz scouts, attacking six of these over Jenin aerodrome and forcing all six down. Ten days later two F2Bs crewed by Lts Peters and Traill, and McGinness and Fletcher engaged a total of eight enemy aircraft and destroyed four; while on 31 August Lts McGinness and Fysh attacked two LVGs west of Mulebbis; Hudson Fysh destroyed both of them, one German

Left:
F2B B1146 with its crew of Capt Ross Smith (right) and Lt E. A. Mustard of No 1 Squadron AFC.

Right:
Ross Smith and E. A. Mustard ready to go, in F2B B1229. *Late Air Marshal Sir R. Williams, RAAF*

aircraft falling in British territory and the other at Kalkilieh.

While No 1 Squadron's F2Bs were wreaking havoc upon the enemy during August 1918, Gen Allenby was finalising his plans for one final, all-out offensive which might totally oust the Turkish armies. By the end of that month Allenby's operational preparations were completed and the offensive was ordered to be launched on 19 September. For its part in the scheme No 1 Squadron was accorded the honour of overall strategic bombing and reconnaissance, and general 'supervisors' of the battle areas. On 29 August an addition to the squadron's strength in the shape of a Handley Page 0/400, C9681, arrived at Ramleh — the sole example in the theatre — and on 19 September — the opening day of the Battle of Nablus, more commonly referred to as the Battle of the Fields of Armageddon — the huge Handley Page, with a bomb load of 16 112lb bombs and piloted by Ross Smith, wrecked the enemy's central telephone exchange at El Afule and the nearby rail junction. Later that evening Ross Smith took off in the 0/400 and this time dropped his bombs on Jenin aerodrome and its adjacent rail station. Meantime the Turkish armies began to retreat — the start of what was to become a horrifying massacre of Turkish troops and transports over the ensuing few days, in a true second Armegeddon.

First air reports of the main Turkish retreat came from two F2Bs, B1284 (Capt A. R. Brown and Lt G. Findlay) and B1285 (Lts S. A. Nunan and F. C. Conrick), who radioed back on the morning of 21 September that enemy transport was moving back via the Balata/Ferweh/Shibleh/Jordan road, along Wadi Beidan — a valley with steep hills on one side and a sheer precipice on the other. The two F2Bs then bombed and strafed troops at zero height, creating many casualties. Thereafter, throughout the day, relays of RAF aircraft from all squadrons kept up a relentless and unmerciful slaughter of the trapped Turkish columns; first bombing the head of the columns and thereby effectively blocking any further escape, then cutting a swathe of death and destruction through the congested thousands of Turkish troops. The carnage outstripped imagination, and by the end of that day most Bristol F2B crews (and no doubt of other units involved) were appalled by the mass killing. As one Australian summed up his own reactions; 'It was sheer butchery . . . we were a tough bunch, but we were sickened . . . in two days over what became the Nine Miles of Dead, our squadron dropped three tons of bombs and fired 30,000 machine gun rounds. We, of No 1 Squadron, were the chief butchers; the RAF squadrons between them only dropped and fired the same quantity'. (*Aces and Kings*, by L. Sutherland; J. Hamilton, 1936.) It was the graveyard of the Turkish Seventh and Eighth Armies, though the aerial onslaught continued thereafter as the surviving Turks were further harassed in their head-long retreat.

As the RAF decimated Turkish troops in the 'Valley of Death', No 1 Squadron was asked to assist the Arab northern army, inspired by T. E. Lawrence, and therefore despatched three F2Bs to the Arab 'HQ' at Um es Surab, primarily to deal with the German aircraft based at Deraa which had been attacking Lawrence's Arab forces. These F2Bs, plus the giant Handley Page 0/400, arrived at Um es Surab early on 22 September and shortly after 10.00hrs B1229 (Capt Ross Smith and Lt Mustard) and B1295 (Lts E. S. Headlam and W. H. Lilly) shot down a DFW two-seater, then attacked three enemy scouts and drove all three down. In the afternoon B1278 (Lts Peters and Traill) forced a DFW down smoking near its airfield and then destroyed it with Lewis gun fire. Early next morning C4626 and C4627 from Ramleh dropped 16 bombs across Deraa airfield, setting a hangar afire and destroying or damaging several DFWs; and that night the Handley Page rounded out the attacks by dropping nearly a ton of bombs on Deraa. No more opposition came from Deraa aerodrome for the remaining weeks of the war.

Allenby continued his advance towards Damascus, with the RAF units continuing their harrying of the retreating enemy troops, No 1 Squadron attacking troop columns on the Es Salt-Amman road on 23 September with 48 bombs and 7,000 rounds in the early part of the day, then concentrating on Amman where a total of almost three tons of bombs and 15,000 rounds were expended by nightfall. This was to be the daily pattern of operations for No 1 Squadron's F2B crews thereafter — bombing and strafing enemy troops wherever they could be caught in the open. In the afternoon of 28 September four F2Bs raided Damascus aerodrome, and next day the airfield was reported as evacuated by Germans. On 30 September one F2B crew, Lts Maughan and Weir, came upon a remnant force of about 4,000 infantry and cavalry scattered along the north bank of the Zabirani and dived to attack. The Turks, too exhausted and dispirited to even move, sat in resignation, and out of pity the F2B crew refrained from firing. Next day British cavalry entered Damascus to find no sign of the enemy in the city except for abandoned stores and equipment. In the following days No 1 Squadron left Ramleh to move to Haifa from where it could carry out long-range recce sorties searching for the remaining enemy forces. On 19 October two F2Bs, B1229 (Ross Smith and McCann) and B1295 (Lts Headlam and Lilly), met the first German aircraft seen since the attacks on Deraa, a DFW CV, which they forced to land and then set fire to by a Very light cartridge. Finally, on 23 October, No 1 Squadron had its last action involving German aircraft when during an attack on Muslimie, north of Aleppo, Lts S. H. Harper and Lilly chased two DFWs down to the nearby aerodrome where four more two-seaters were seen apparently about to take-off. The F2B attacked all six German aircraft with bombs, then flew to and fro strafing them with machine guns. Not one German attempted to rise to this cheeky challenge.

An armistice on 31 October brought the war against Turkey to an end. No 1 Squadron AFC moved back to Ramleh in December, then to Kantara, Egypt in February 1919, from where, on 5 March 1919, the squadron left the deserts aboard SS *Port Sydney*, bound for Australia. The unit's faithful Bristol F2Bs had been transferred en bloc to No 111 Squadron RAF at Ramleh in February, but not before one Australian pilot had persuaded the No 111 Squadron commander to allow him one last flip in an F2B. Circling Ramleh aerodrome, the F2B, C4626, dipped a wing in salute, then scattered a handful of Palestine poppies — the final tribute to the squadron's dead.

Left:
Capt Sir Ross Smith KBE, DFC, AFC, the 'star turn' of No 1 Squadron AFC, who was knighted postwar for an epic flight from England to Australia in November-December 1919. He died in a flying accident near Brooklands, England on 13 April 1922.

In Italian Skies

On 24 October 1917 the Austro-German armies launched a strong offensive against the Italian armies and quickly broke Italian resistance at Caporetto. Thrusting forward, the Austro-German forces swept rapidly west and southwestwards until by 10 November they were on the banks of the River Piave, having advanced 50-80 miles at the deepest point. Here, due to insufficient reserves immediately available to exploit this victory, the Austro-German troops paused, but remained an imminent threat to Italian territories while they rebuilt their strength. This potentially disastrous situation for Britain's ally, Italy, led the British and French goverments to agree on 26 October to send divisions from the Western Front quickly, with air support from Nos 28 (Sopwith Camels) and 34 (RE8s) Squadrons, units transferred from France; these squadrons began their move from France on 7 November. Further agreement was reached on 5 November to supplement these forces by two more divisions and two more RAF units, Nos 45 and 66 Squadrons (Camels), and soon after a third RAF unit, No 42 Squadron (RE8s). By the end of November 1917 all the RAF units transferred from France were established at forward airfields and ready for operations, with the first RAF sortie over the Italian front being flown on 29 November by Capt Thompson in an RE8 of No 34 Squadron, attempting to photograph enemy dispositions in the Montello area. The RE8 was attacked by five enemy scouts but escaped unscathed, while a few days later a second RE8 (Capt Pirrie MC) was beset by seven enemy scouts and also evaded these successfully.

By February 1918 the presence of the RAF squadrons alongside the Italian air service had re-established Allied superiority in the air along the Italian front, but Nos 34 and 43 Squadrons' RE8s rarely flew long-range reconnaissance sorties without fierce opposition from the enemy fighters, and therefore had to be escorted by the Camel units. To rectify this situation a Flight of Bristol

Below:
A line-up of No 139 Squadron at Villaverla, Italy in mid-1918. The two white bars on the fuselages was the initial unit marking, but was later expanded. Nearest is F2B D8063 'D', which arrived on the squadron on 26 July 1918.

Above:
F2B D7966 'A' arrived on No 139 Squadron on 16 August 1918, but was lost on 23 August (Lts C. E. G. Gill and T. Newey), and is seen here in Austrian hands after capture. Note that the Squadron marking is now four white bars on the rear fuselage. *Via G. Stuart Leslie*

F2Bs, formed in England in March 1918 under the command of Capt T. C. Lowe MC, was sent to the Italian front in the same month, being initially attached as a fourth Flight to No 28 Squadron, but then transferred to No 34 Squadron at Istrana airfield, just west of Treviso, where it became titled 'Z' Flight. The Bristol F2Bs then took over responsibility for all long-range recces from the RE8s — though the latter had flown such sorties for four months without a single aircraft loss to enemy fighters — and on 30 March No 34 Squadron with its 'Z' Flight moved base to Villaverla. From here the F2Bs commenced single-aircraft recce sorties, but after one such recce F2B failed to return on 3 April fighter escorts of three to six Sopwith Camels accompanied the F2Bs thereafter. Even so, occasional solo recces continued to be flown by 'Z' Flight, resulting in another F2B loss (B1212) on 25 April.

Throughout April and May 1918 weather conditions over the mountainous front were often too bad for any flying or successful reconnaissance, but from what evidence that was gathered it appeared that another enemy offensive might soon be launched in the Val Sugana area. To forestal such a move the Allied commanders in mid-May decided to prepare their own offensive on the Asiago front — only to be forced to postpone such intention when increased activity along the Piave areas gave even stronger indications of a forthcoming Austrian offensive. Attempts to uncover Austrian intentions met with hardy resistance by the Austro-Hungarian air services, and on 10 May Oberleutnant Frank Linke-Crawford, commander of the Austrian *Flik 60* fighter squadron, shot down F2B C4755 (Lts J. B. Guthrie and H. Y. Thornton) near Levico, killing both crewmen. On 2 June an F2B crew, 2/Lts Brown and Milburn, attacked five Albatroses over Borgo and claimed one shot down out of control, while on 9 June three F2Bs undertook a recce and were attacked by six Albatroses. Of these, 2/Lts A. E. Ryan and T. Newey shot one Albatros down in flames, while Lts Robertson and Milburn claimed a second 'Driven down', but a third F2B was forced down by Feldwebel Alexander Kasza of *Flik 55J*. On the same day Capt T. C. Lowe and 2/Lt A. S. Withers in F2B C913 were both wounded and crashed on landing at Villaverla.

On 15 June the expected Austrian offensive was launched along the whole front from east of Astico to the sea, preceded by a brief but heavy artillery bombardment. All RAF units joined in the strenuous efforts to stem this advance, and low-level bombing and strafing of enemy troops, bridges, river traffic, even rafts became the order of the day, as Austrian forces poured across the River Piave. The RAF and Italian airmen's immediate reaction created huge slaughter among the enemy troops crossing the Piave, thereby

imposing delays in the initial stages of the enemy offensive and causing wide confusion and disruption of Austrian plans. Two days later heavy rains converted the Piave river into a swirling torrent, washing away all Austrian temporary pontoon bridges and isolating troops on either side of the river. An Italian counter-offensive led to desperate fighting for several days, but by 20 June Austrian troops were being slowly pushed back to the Piave, and two days later these were ordered to withdraw across the river. By 24 June this withdrawal had been accomplished but at a cost of 20,000 troops captured apart from a large number of guns and other vital material equipment. Though it would be exaggerating to claim that the RAF's prompt reaction had been the key to the Allies' success in repulsing this Austrian advance, it should be acknowledged that the air support had been a vital factor in halting then disorganising the opening phases of that offensive, giving the Italian, British and French troops time to assemble their counter-attack.

At the end of June 1918 a second Flight of Bristol F2Bs arrived from England to reinforce 'Z' Flight, but on 28 June Lts Williams and Thomas in F2B C993 received a direct hit from anti-aircraft fire and crashed in flames near San Polo. On 3 July the F2Bs of 'Z' Flight were officially retitled No 139 Squadron RAF, still based at Villaverla under the continuing command of Capt A. A. Harcourt-Vernon, and on the following day duly celebrated the new status when three F2Bs on a recce sortie tackled four Albatroses and claimed two as victories. On 15 July command of No 139 Squadron was invested in the capable hands of the noted Canadian Maj W. G. Barker DSO, MC,

Above:
No 139 Squadron personnel in the summer of 1918. Standing (left to right): Lts Foster; Hill; Winter; Milburn; Exton; Jellicoe and Horner; Capt Hursthouse; Maj W. G. Barker DSO, MC, (OC Squadron); Capt S. Dalrymple DFC; Lts Bartram; Dowse; Crump; Forbes and Johnson. Seated (left to right): Lts Abram; ?; Lewis; G. W. Curtis; W. C. Simon; Austin; Geyton and Wallace. On wing: 2/Lt Kaye (left). Behind them is Barker's personal Sopwith Camel, B6313.

who had been promoted and transferred from No 66 Squadron, and brought with him his personal warhorse, Sopwith Camel B6313. Next day four F2Bs took off in the early morning for a recce, though one machine soon returned with engine problems. The other three sighted and attacked eight enemy aircraft over Mattarello and shot down two to crash, while on 16 July two more victories were claimed. Two days later George Barker set out in his Camel, B6313, accompanied by an F2B (Lts H. C. Walters and W. T. Davies), and the two machines engaged two two-seaters escorted by three scouts over Asiago. Barker quickly shot down one of the two-seaters, an LVG, which crashed — his first confirmed victory as OC, No 139 Squadron. On 20 July Barker was again airborne in his Camel, leading two F2Bs, and shot down two Albatros scouts near Motta airfield, while one of the F2B crews, Lt G. W. Curtis and Sgt H. G. Frow, despatched a third Albatros. On 23 July Lts H. C. Walters and Davies destroyed another Austrian aircraft over its own airfield at

Godega, but on the same day two lone F2Bs flying separate recces failed to return — Lt W. L. Vorster and Sgt H. G. Frow in F2B C4759 and Lts V. D. Fernald and W. C. Watkins in C4762 falling victims to Friedrich Navratil of *Flimk 3J* and Oberleutnant Roman Schmidt of *Flik 30J*.

On 30 July a recce sortie by three F2Bs, led by Capt Sidney Dalrymple MC, encountered a formation of two Austrian two-seaters and seven Albatros scouts between Motta and Portogruaro. In the ensuing dogfight Lt W. C. Simon and Lt W. W. Smith in F2B C999 claimed three Albatros and two two-seaters as shot down, despite Smith being wounded part way through the clash. Since at least four of Simon and Smith's victims were reported as 'in flames' or 'crashed', it is curious that Austrian records admit no air casualties on that date. Next day the crew of F2B C990 — Lts R. L. Evans and A. E. Ryan — were both wounded in combat, while on 1 August F2B D8081 was crashed on an Italian airfield during gunnery practice by its crew of Lts Ramsey and Crump — this aircraft having only arrived on the squadron the day previous! On 8 August a trio of F2Bs left Villaverla for a routine reconnaissance patrol, led by Sidney Dalrymple and his Observer, Lt Baldwin in F2B D8084 'S'. Dalrymple first attacked an Albatros scout over Trento but the Austrian spun down to 6,000ft and then recovered and left the area. Later Dalrymple spotted two more Albatroses near Levico and he and his gunner each claimed a victim, their adversaries being Karl Linner and Johann Pinkalsky from *Flik 9J* who were — ironically — engaged on a protection patrol above Austrian airfields in the area because of a royal visit by Emperor Carl to aerodromes in that vicinity. Another member of Dalrymple's patrol, Lt W. C. Simon, also claimed to have 'driven down' a two-seater, and two days later, flying D8075, Simon, with Sgt Akam as his gunner, attacked a pair of Albatros scouts over Caldonazzo and shot one down to crash in a wood.

Still pursuing the offensive spirit of the squadron, Dalrymple led four F2Bs on a bombing raid against Levico airfield on 16 August, but lost one of his quartet when F2B D8069 (Lts C. R. H. Jackson and Keepin) was shot down in flames over Trento by Oberleutnant Navratil, commander of the Austrian *Flik 3J*, as his eighth credited victory. On 23 August Navratil was to claim another F2B for his ninth *Luftsieg* when he forced down D7966 (Lts C. E. G. Gill and T. Newey) at Gardolo, its crew becoming prisoners of war: their aircraft, captured intact, had only arrived on No 139 Squadron on 16 August. The day before this action another F2B crew, Lts Gwyer and Hilton flying D8075, were shot down by Feldwebel Karl Teichmann of *Flik 14J* to become prisoners of the Austrians. For the remainder of August and early September No 139 Squadron's daily activities comprised mainly reconnaissance and photographic sorties, with only sporadic clashes with Austro-Hungarian airmen, but on 13 September came a clash which produced several combat victories for the F2B crews. Led by Sidney

Below:
HRH Prince Edward of Wales (later HM King Edward VIII) about to have a local 'flip' in F2B 'S', D8084 of No 139 Squadron. His pilot here is unidentified but was *not* Maj George Barker on this occasion, despite repeated assertions in past publications.

Below:
Maj Barker piloting F2B D8063 'D' of No 139 Squadron over Villaverla with HRH Prince Edward in the rear cockpit.
Public Archives of Canada: C-59872

Dalrymple, four F2Bs sighted 10 Albatros scouts over Trento at some 15,000ft and promptly engaged these. Dalrymple dived on one Albatros and sent it down flaming, but was then beset by another Albatros. His gunner, Lt Beagle, used up three drums of ammunition on this antagonist before it erupted in flames and fell to destruction. Meanwhile Lt Curtis sent one Albatros down 'Out of control', then shot down a second pluming flames, while his gunner, Air Mechanic Ings, shot a third Albatros spinning down out of control. Next day Lt J. B. Isaacs claimed an Albatros when his close-range fire caused the scout to break up in mid-air. For the next few days the F2B crews concentrated on low-level bombing raids against various Austrian aerodromes at Levico and Fonzaso, and adjacent railway stations, apart from strafing attacks against enemy troop locations.

On 20 September F2B D7972 was crashed near Terognano by Lt E. Exton and AM Hare — an aircraft in which HRH Prince Edward (later King Edward VIII) had been given local flights by Maj Barker four days before — but six days later Lts H. V. Jellicoe and A. MacKay sent an Albatros down to crash south of Lavis. At the start of October all RAF squadrons began bombing and strafing attacks specifically against Austrian airfields, paying particular attention to the training aerodromes at Campoformido, southwest of Udine, and Egna, south of Bolzano, and Pergine; the latter was bombed by No 139 Squadron on 7 October to good effect. Next day four F2Bs engaged on a recce were jumped by nine Albatros over Borgo and the leading F2B, D7957 (Capt S. H. Holland and 2/Lt R. G. Fullager) came under heavy attack leaving Fullager wounded and Holland's front gun jammed. Nevertheless, Fullager kept firing at one Albatros which fell away spinning viciously then dived vertically into the ground.

By this time the command of No 139 Squadron had passed temporarily to Capt Sidney Dalrymple following Maj Barker's repatriation to England on 30 September, and he remained in command until 23 October when Maj H. H. Kitchener (a nephew of Field Marshal Lord Kitchener) arrived to assume his offical appointment as unit CO. Meanwhile plans for a final offensive against the Austro-Hungarian armies were well in hand by Gen Diaz, Italian C-in-C, and as part of the preceding re-alignment of the RAF support units, No 139 Squadron left Villaverla on 9 October, moving its base to Grossa airfield, northwest of Padua. From here its crews were frustrated by bad weather from attempting any photo-reconnaissance sorties for several days, but once the weather improved an intense programme of photo recces was instigated, with the squadron's photographic section producing no less than 8,000 photographic prints for the army commanders in the 48-hour period 22-24 October alone. Then, on Sunday 27 October, the Allied offensive commenced at 06.45hrs, and No 139 Squadron's F2Bs joined the remaining RAF units in offensive patrols, claiming an Austrian scout shot down south of Mareno by Lts A. Bartram and C. Sander but being primarily concerned in zero-height bombing and machine gunning the Austro-Hungarian infantry positions.

Within three days the Austrian armies were in full retreat, verging on a complete rout, constantly harried by Allied aircraft bombing and strafing their retreating troop columns and destroying transports. Inevitably, perhaps, casualties were suffered by the aircrews from ground fire, as on 30 October when Maj Kitchener, with Lt H. Dowse as gunner, was recipient of some accurate ground fire which wounded Dowse in a leg, while on the same day Capt L. F. Hursthouse and Lt W. W. Smith in F2B D7969 also suffered hits, wounding Hursthouse in his chest and leading to a crash landing. Dowse, tragically, went into hospital for treatment to his leg but then became a victim of virulent influenza and died on Armistice Day. Following up the rapid Allied advance No 139 Squadron left Grossa on 1 November and moved to Arcade, just south of the Piave river, but by then it was apparent that the war in Italy was virtually over. Even so, the RAF squadrons maintained their unrelenting offensive against the routed Austrians up until the enemy surrender, and the official cessation of hostilities on 4 November. In its relatively brief existence No 139 Squadron had flown a total of just over 1,450 hours on operations, dropped nearly five and a half tons of bombs, and in air combat had claimed totals of 25 enemy aircraft destroyed, seven others 'Out of control', apart from others 'Driven down'; to which might be added at least two more enemy aircraft shot down by its 'parent' 'Z' Flight's F2B crews. Its own casualties amounted to 12 aircraft lost in combat, but in the immediate post-armistice euphoria three more F2Bs were wrecked in crashes: D8072 (9 November), E2186 (9 November) and E2292 (7 November). On 14 November the squadron moved back to its former airfield at Grossa, but on 7 March 1919 the squadron was officially disbanded at the Caldiero Aircraft Park.

Below:
F2B D8084 'S' of No 139 Squadron at Villaverla in September 1918 with Capt Sydney Dalrymple in the pilot's seat. Apart from the Charlie Chaplin caricature painted below the engine exhaust, the unit marking of (first) two, then four white bars has now been expanded further, with black bars in between, and two white bars painted all across the upper wing from roundel to roundel.

American Fiasco

When, on 6 April 1917, the United States of America entered the war against Germany, its army's aviation section comprised 131 officers, 1,087 enlisted men and a motley collection of less than 250 aircraft, none of which could seriously have been even considered for combat roles in Europe. Moreover, no specific planned programme for building an air service capable of participating in the European conflict had been prepared. This general lack of up-to-date organisation or even knowledge of the requirements for a combat-worthy air arm was not entirely the fault of American authorities. In the preceding three years of war Allied officialdom had placed a strict embargo on aeronautical information to 'outside' countries, even to the extent of (officially, at least . . .) prohibiting visits to the Western Front by American aviation observers. Yet, once America had committed herself to active involvement in the war, Britain and France immediately pressed hard for the USA to expand and multiply its aviation potential, having in mind particularly the enormous industrial capacity of America for mass production of war materials.

With characteristic whole-hearted enthusiasm and determination the American government reacted swiftly to the situation and drafted a production programme of '22,625 aeroplanes plus 80% spares, and 44,000 engines' (sic); towards which ambitious project the US Congress voted a sum of $640million on 24 July 1917 purely for military aeronautics. In practical terms this bounteous sum enabled the US Army Aviation Section to obtain approval for a target strength of 345 combat squadrons — 263 of which were intended for employment in France by June 1918 — apart from over 100 'support' units of varying types including 26 balloon companies. Meanwhile the Bolling Commission had gone to France in June 1917; its terms of reference being to recommend to the US Government for production the best types of aircraft available in the British, French and Italian combat aviation forces. On 1 August Gen Pershing authorised cables to the

Below:

Curtiss-built USA-0-1 with Liberty engine, seen on 3 March 1918.

USA outlining the commission's final recommendations, among which was the specific request that the Bristol F2B, *with the 200hp Hispano Suiza engine* (author's italics), be built in quantity. Two weeks later, on 14 August, a first 'sample' F2B (A7206) left London bound for the USA and eventually reached Washington on 5 September, ostensibly to act as a pattern for American production designers.

As this 'sample' arrived in Washington, a Col V. E. Clark, freshly arrived home from France, with a small staff of designers and draughtsmen, was allocated the Airplane Exhibition building (a temporary hangar at the rear of the Smithsonian Institute) and tasked with *re*-designing the Bristol F2B to accept the American Liberty-12 aero engine. To quote from a letter sent by Clark to the Director of Military Aeronautics, dated 12 August 1918:

'I was assigned the task of redesigning the Bristol fighter for the Liberty engine. I was given six weeks' working time, very poor facilities, and practically no experienced draftsmen (sic) with which to do the job. At the end of this time, November 1917, I turned over some 880 drawings made in my department for the new design to the Curtiss Airplane Company. Since that date I have never been called upon to visit the Curtiss factory, nor have I ever been consulted in any way regarding questions connected with the design or construction. I believe that an official diary kept by Mr J. G. Perrin, who was designated as the Government Engineering Representative for this job, will show conclusively that the machine as finally flown experimentally, was in no way similar to the machine that my department designed. The same diary will, I believe, show conclusively the reason for the failure of the Bristol Fighter as flown in this country.

'I designed it to be an Observation machine weighing, fully loaded with all necessary equipment, 2,940lbs. There was built a machine which weighed some 700 or 800lbs more, with changes throughout. The machine that was flown was not the machine designed.'

Clark's presentation of his redesign drawings to the Curtiss firm was in accordance with a Government contract awarded to Curtiss in October 1917 for 1,000 F2Bs — fitted with the 400hp Liberty engine — in which guise its American title was designated as USA 0-1 (though the name Bristol Fighter became its commonly used name anyway). On 1 November 1917 the British 'sample' was shipped from Washington express to Curtiss, arriving at the factory on 7 November, and by 23 November sufficient redesign blueprints had been transferred to Curtiss to enable the company to start work on a first machine. On 7 December the original contract for 1,000 machines was cancelled in favour of a fresh contract for 2,000 machines, these to be completed by August 1918. Production lines were set up in the new Elmwood Plant in Buffalo and the Curtiss manufacturing began. To comply with the contract specifications, Curtiss necessarily altered all parts' dimensions to fall in line with existing American tooling and jigging standards, while the intention of employing the Liberty engine meant a complete redesign of the forward fuselage. From the outset the production of the 'Liberty-F2B' was to be beset by a series of additional redesigning in attempts to comply with a variety of requirements foisted upon the designers, including a literal doubling of machine gun and ammunition armament with consequent redesigns of virtually the whole front end of the machine and an all-round beefing up of airframe strength to accommodate such extra warload weights.

Far left:
The American XB-1A F2B variant developed at McCook Field in 1918-19.

Left:
USA-0-1, with radiator on the upper wing centre-section.

There can be little doubt that the prime factor in the eventual dismal saga of the 'American F2B' was the original ill-considered decision to design it around the American-designed Liberty-12 engine. This all-American powerplant had been conceived in May 1917 as an engine design which would incorporate the best features of all contemporary engines, and capable of being produced with four, six, eight or 12 cylinders to power a variety of aircraft designs. With typical American high-powered industriousness the first example of this new engine was completed on 3 July 1917 and rushed to Washington by the next day — Independence Day — hence its given title Liberty. This first example had eight cylinders, but a 12-cylinder version was already in hand and had completed a 50-hour bench test by 25 August. Its introduction, amid much ballyhoo propaganda publicity, led to highly optimistic production forecast figures — by May 1918 monthly output was confidently expected to be 4,800, with a gross total of 9,420 to be manufactured by the end of that month. In the event little more than 1,000 Liberty engines had actually been completed by 25 May. Based on the initial forecast, Britain's interest in the Liberty was indicated by orders totalling 3,000 engines by January 1918, which month, the manufacturers promised, would see the start of monthly deliveries of 500; these were intended to power the forthcoming de Havilland 9A bombers. Nevertheless, when the Bristol Co was told of the intention to instal the Liberty in American-produced F2Bs, Frank Barnwell was horrified and protested such an idea, only to be over-ruled despite his prediction of plentiful problems should the idea be adopted.

The doubts of several aeronautical experts in Britain and France about a Liberty-engined F2B were emphatically denied by US officialdom and on 27 February 1918 Gen Pershing sent a cable back to Washington, quoting '50 squadrons of F2Bs are contemplated'. In the interim the Curtiss production programme had been placed under the aegis of Maj E. J. Hall for the Equipment Division of the US Army Signal Corps. Hall, along with Col Jesse G. Vincent, had been a co-developer of the Liberty engine, hence Hall's appointment to the F2B programme in February 1918. The first F2B completed by Curtiss on 25 January 1918 soon exhibited problems with its engine installation and Maj Hall initiated sweeping changes in the existing design — thereby rendering almost 1,400 existing Signal Corps drawings obsolete — in order to incorporate extra equipment and raise the design's safety factor. In a letter dated 19 April 1918 to M. W. Kellogg, Director of Production, Hall complained:

'I do not know who was responsible for the adaptation of this [the original F2B supplied by Britain] machine, or for the original sample that was built from the design, but I do know that the Curtiss Co greatly opposed building this machine as designed. The Liberty engine was much too large and too powerful for the plane without thoroughly redesigning and strengthening it all the way thru. The design furnished was of the crudest type and the plane would scarcely stand up on its own weight on the floor. It was not designed, nor any provision made, to carry any type of equipment whatsoever. . . . When this writer was called upon to put this plane into production, it was already so far along, it was necessary to strengthen up the main points in best manner possible. The first 400 machines so strengthened were released to Curtiss for production, and they will be fairly good machines and very serviceable. It was not as good a job as could be made so the writer, in conjunction with the Engineering Department of the Curtiss Company, completely redesigned the machine as a two-seater, pursuit type, equipped with oxygen tanks, forward Marlin guns and two Lewis machine guns in the Observer's cockpit. With this class of equipment, it is confidently expected that the new machine will make 150 miles per hour, and be superior to anything that is over on the other side. Machine must not carry anything else, and is not suitable for bombing, camera, or radio gun-spotting work.'

Hall's criticism of Clark's original design drawings were, apparently, justified; while subsequent Signal Corps' additional equipment requirements took the all-up weight from 2,900lb to 4,000lb. Meanwhile the first Curtiss F2B was undergoing further tests, and in April 1918 a second machine was built quickly, in just six days, from available equipment at Curtiss purely as an experimental machine to prove the balance of the design and the viability of using the Liberty engine. This stripped-down F2B was air-tested at Dayton by Lt Jimmy Doolittle (pilot) and Lt W. M. Oler (Observer) on 7 May, but at the top of its third test loop fabric peeled away from the upper port wing and only Doolittle's skill in 'force-landing' on a nest of telegraph wires saved his and Oler's lives. It might be added that Doolittle's private opinion of the design was succinctly expressed when, the evening before the flight, he gave a fellow officer a copy of his will for safekeeping. . . . In France, however, Pershing was still 'contemplating' the promised F2B squadrons for the American airmen there, his optimism being boosted slightly by receipt of a cable on 1 April 1918 which informed him that he could expect the following monthly totals of F2B *squadrons*: May, one; June, four; July, nine; August, nine; September, three; and two more in October 1918, ie a total of 28 complete F2B squadrons within six months. On 27 April Curtiss finished its first four production machines, and the first pair of these went to Wilbur Wright Field on 5 May to be set up; on 1 May Colonel (as he was by now) Hall completed his redesigning of the F2B as a fighter, now armed with four Marlin machine guns forward and a single Lewis for its Observer, and work began on four sample machines of this design to be ready for air-testing by 1 June.

At this stage an undercurrent of worried criticism of the whole Liberty-F2B programme was swelling, and in late May 1918 Capt Henry — 'Hap' — Arnold recommended to the Chief of the Equipment Division, USSC that Frank Barnwell be requested to design a new aircraft around the Liberty engine, a view supported by the head of that Division, Col T. H. Bane, who wrote, 'No one in this country is as capable of handling the situation as the original designer, Capt Barnwell'. Considering Barnwell's original strongly expressed views on the subject, this latest move by US authorities was somewhat ironic. These 'second thoughts' by certain of the American hierarchy were reflected in an Air Service Program dated 14 May 1918 which, among other items, called for the F2B to be fitted with the 300hp Hispano Suiza engine instead of the Liberty, a proposition later to be taken up at high level. Then, on 10 June, a second F2B crashed with fatal consequences when Lt Philip Rader (pilot) and Robert Conner (Observer) were on an air-test over the Curtiss field. At about 3pm fabric was seen to peel away from the port upper wing, the F2B fell into a nose-dive, then plunged from 500ft straight into the earth, its petrol tank exploding on impact and totally destroying crew and machine. Rader, like Doolittle, was no novice and therefore the only possible conclusion was of defects in the aircraft design. Little more than four weeks later, on 15 July, a third F2B crash occurred when Lt Sharp (pilot), and his Observer, Lt Hale, lost control of their aircraft after recovering from a barrel roll manoeuvre and crashed, burning out, killing Sharp and seriously injuring Hale.

Three days later a conference decision was made to halt production of the Liberty-F2B, and next day a cable was despatched to Gen Pershing advising: 'Liberty-12 F2B is . . . not of military value, therefore (is) to be abandoned and exact copy of English Bristol, with 300hp Hispano instead.' Accordingly, on 20 July, the Curtiss contract was cancelled (effective cancellation date to be 30 September 1918); a contract cancellation which was calculated at a cost of $6,482,000. Thus between April and July 1918 total Curtiss production had been merely 26 machines. The projected 300hp Hispano Suiza-engined F2B plan gathered some momentum when, on 2 October 1918, the Aircraft Board authorised a production order for 2,000 such F2Bs, but by the end of the same month advice had been received from England that Bristol Fighters were '. . . no longer fitted with 300hp Hispano, therefore impossible to obtain drawings for this engine mounting'. It was the deathblow for a highly ambitious scheme to 'marry' the well-tried Bristol F2B and the (then) unproven Liberty engine, but the Air Service Engineering Division at McCook Field developed a lower-powered variant F2B, taking two Bristol-built aircraft and installing a 300hp Hispano Suiza in one (titled P.30), and a 290hp Liberty-8 in the other (P.37). The latter aircraft crashed before providing any performance test figures, but the P.30 established an unofficial world altitude record of 29,800ft over Dayton on 18 November 1918, piloted by a Maj Schroeder. A further McCook Field variant to be built was P.90 (US designation XB-1A) in July 1919, powered by a 300hp Wright-Hispano engine, with its fuselage of semi-monocoque, laminated wood veneer. This proved reasonably successful and a further 30 such 'F2Bs' were produced in 1920 by the Dayton-Wright Aircraft Co, still with the designation XB-1A.

Technical Data, USA 0-1 F2B

Span: 39ft 4in
Length: 27ft 1in
Height: 10ft 2in
Wing area: 416sq ft
Weight empty: 2,245lb
Weight gross: 3,500lb
Max speed: 125mph (sea level)
Climb to 10,000ft: 7.05 minutes
Absolute ceiling: 25,000ft
Endurance: 2 hours
Armament: 2×Marlin MG forward; 2×Lewis MG rear

Above left:
The P-30 version of the American F2B.

Left:
A P-37 F2B, with 290hp Liberty 8 engine.

Above:
The first US-XB-1A, seen in 1919. SC-40125, serial P-90 and with semi-monocoque fuselage, was developed at McCook Field.

Post-Armistice, UK and Foreign

When hostilities in Europe ceased somewhat abruptly in November 1918, the British aviation production programmes, in parallel with those of the USA, France and Italy, were gaining huge momentum in sheer quantity and had already created sizeable stocks of aircraft, engines and myriad accessories. Thus, with the near-immediate reduction in strength of the RAF and its allied air services, a large surplus of new, operationally ready aircraft became available for purchase by various European countries already planning future military air forces. The well-established reputation of the Bristol F2B (among other prominent RAF designs) led to several such European countries purchasing F2Bs for first-line squadron use. One such country, with a particularly urgent need for military aircraft, was Poland. After being partitioned between Russia, Germany and Austria-Hungary for more than a century, Poland emerged as an independent state in the autumn of 1918, only to spend the following two years fighting a succession of campaigns against armed Russian occupation. The Polish Air Force was created as a single unified command in December 1918, equipped with ex-Austrian and ex-German aircraft 'acquired' during the latter months of 1918; but the bulk of these were unsuitable for operational work.

By 1920 the crucial need for more military aircraft resulted in large orders being placed with France, Italy and Great Britain, the latter presenting Poland with (initially) 12 de Havilland

Below:
An F2B bearing ex-RAF serial H1279 and Polish serial 20.48. *A. Morgala Collection*

Above:
Two views of Polish F2B 20.71, illustrating the Polish national red and white markings.
Both T. Goworek

Below:
Canadian F2B G-CYBC (ex-RAF serial F4336, an ex-presentation aircraft titled successively *Zanzibar 17* then *Huddersfield*). It is seen here at Rockcliffe, Ontario, c1922.
Public Archives of Canada: PA-62275

9s and 20 single-seat fighters (Sopwith Dolphins, Camels, SE5As and a Martinsyde F4), and additionally accepting an order for 105 Bristol F2Bs for delivery to Poland in the spring of 1920. (In the event, apart from single-seat fighters, Poland received about 110 F2Bs and 22 DH9s.) Actual deliveries of the promised British aircraft were delayed for several months by British dockers who, incited by communist agitators, refused to handle the Polish aircraft cargoes, and it was not until the first week of August 1920 that these aircraft began reaching Poland, just before the crucial Battle of Warsaw, and Bristol F2Bs in Polish markings went into action for the first time on 14 August. These F2Bs arrived in Warsaw in dismantled state, without any form of technical manuals or assembly instructions, but a few dozen F2Bs were quickly put together by Polish mechanics entirely by instinctive 'feel' (and no little guesswork), and as any F2B appeared completed a waiting aircrew flew it into battle immediately. With no experience of such items as the F2B's tail actuating gear, crashes inevitably occurred, often with crew fatalities, but once the pilots had mastered correct handling the F2Bs gained an excellent reputation. In October 1920 a cease-fire agreement brought hostilities to a halt, and by the end of January 1921 the Polish Air Force had been re-organised to comprise 13 operational squadrons. Of these, three were equipped with F2Bs — Nos 1, 5 and 10 Reconnaissance Squadrons, based at Bialystok Przemysl and Krakow respectively, though actual numbers of serviceable F2Bs on each unit was

Above right:
This F2B (Bristol Construction No 6857) was one of two Mk IIs bought in 1925 for the New Zealand Permanent Air Force (NZPAF). *Via B. Robertson*

Centre right:
F2B '19' of the Irish Free State Army Air Corps, with 260hp Rolls-Royce Falcon III engine, delivered on 20 October 1925.
C. H. Barnes

Below:
The F2B presented to King Albert of the Belgians by the Handley Page Co on 14 May 1920, bearing an appropriate regal insigne.
C. H. Barnes

seldom more than five at any given time. By August 1921 all three F2B squadrons came under the aegis of the 3rd Air Regiment as VII Recce *Dyon*, based at Poznan, but by 1925 F2Bs had been replaced by Potez 15A2 aircraft.

In 1922 the Greek government bought six standard F2Bs, and in the same year Norway purchased five reconditioned ex-RAF F2Bs. On 28 November 1918 the Canadian government requested the return of 14 'presentation' aircraft given to the RAF during the war. Since most of the original aircraft had already been written off, replacements were substituted from aircraft based in France, and included at least five Bristol F2Bs — F4334, F4678, B1186, F4336 and D7869 — of which at least the last two went to Canada where they were registered as G-CYBC and G-CYDP respectively. Two other F2Bs, H1557 and H1558, were included in an Imperial Gift of 20 Avro 504s, nine DH9s and two DH4s to New Zealand as a nucleus for the New Zealand Permanent Air Force which came into being on 14 June 1923, and was later retitled the Royal New Zealand Air Force on 27 February 1934. H1557 ended its career in a crash in the grounds of a Methodist orphanage in Papanui, Christchurch on 17 Marh 1926, killing its pilot, Capt Horrell. By July 1927 five more F2Bs had been delivered to New Zealand. Of these, Bristol seq Nos 6856, 6857 and 7120 left the factory for shipping to New Zealand on 28 August 1925; the remaining pair were Bristol seq Nos 7121 and 7122. (7122 was the 3,576th, and last, F2B built at Bristol for the Air Ministry.) No 7121 failed to pull out of a dive on a firing range at Lake Ellesmere, Christchurch on 25 February 1936, killing Flg Off

Top:
The F2B presented to the Queen of the Belgians, with its former civil UK registration G-EBCU faintly visible. This F2B was originally serialled E2058, and was flown on delivery by A. F. Muir on 17 January 1922 from Croydon to Evere in 84 minutes (take-off to landing).
G. Stuart Leslie

Above:
Bristol F2Bs of the Belgian Air Force at Evere, c1920, with a former German Zeppelin shed in the background. *Lt-Col Avi M. Terlinden BEM*

G. M. Owen. In that year three other F2Bs were still on RNZAF charge at Wigram; nevertheless, no F2Bs appeared on RNZAF strength in 1937 and (it is believed) all surviving F2Bs ended their days ignominiously by being burned on Wigram's dump circa 1938.

Nearer home, the Irish Free State Army eventually bought a total of 14 F2Bs, including H1251 and H1485, in late 1925, and these were given the national markings of 20in wide stripes in green/white/yellow on their wings, with the same colours applied to rudders (green next to the hinge posts). However, the European country which used F2Bs most extensively in the post-Armistice period was Belgium. The first F2B to go to Belgium was a Falcon-powered example, suitably refurbished and given a regal monogram on its fuselage sides, presented as a gift to King Albert by Handley Page Ltd (which owned the Aircraft Disposals Co) on 14 May 1920 and, after special modifications requested by the King, was flown to Brussels on 23 July 1920. By the example of its King, the Belgian government then purchased a total of 15 F2Bs (300hp Hispano Suiza) from the Aircraft Disposals Co, and a further 16 newly-built F2Bs from the Bristol Co (seq Nos 6223-6238), again Hispano-powered. A 'royal' F2B (believed to have been ex-E2058/G-EBCU) was also a gift from the ADC, this time to the Belgian Queen, and was delivered by air from Croydon to Brussels on 17 January 1922. In 1925, having acquired a licence, the firm Societé Anonyme Belge de Constructions Aeronautique (SABCA) built a total of 40 Bristol Fighters, many of these having oleo undercarriages, Frise ailerons, horn-balanced rudders and fins similar to the RAF's standard F2B

Left:
A Belgian F2B as used by the Wevelghem training school.
AELR Museum, Brussels

Below left:
F2B F4717 of No 2 Squadron RAF, which was later converted to Mk IV standard. The fuselage bands were contemporary unit marking of two outer red bands, with the centre band in Flight colours of white ('A'), yellow ('B') or blue ('C' Flight).
Late W. E. Johns

Above:
F2B H1460, the first passenger-conversion, was sold to the Air Board on 19 May 1919 and subsequently attached to No 24 Squadron RAF.
Bristol Aeroplane Co

Centre right:
F2Bs on No 24 (VIP) Squadron RAF in July 1919, with H1460, a 'Coupe' variant, nearest.
G. Stuart Leslie

Right:
F2B E2624 'A-4' of No 4 Squadron RAF demonstrating the message pick-up hook method of army co-operation communication.

Below:
E2645 of No 48 Squadron at Bickendorf in the winter of 1918-19. Its presentation inscription read *Allerton-Bywater.* *RAF Museum P1307*

Mk IV, and 300hp Hispano Suiza engines. Some of these F2Bs were still in service in 1930 at the Wevelghem elementary flying school. Bristol F2Bs also found their ways to various other countries around the globe, including Holland, Peru and Mexico — the latter buying 10 machines (Bristol seq Nos 7222-7231) in 1928 — while one F2B was even reported as in service with Sun Yat Sen's rebel forces in China!

In the United Kingdom the year 1919 witnessed a rapid rundown of F2B squadrons (among many others) but the following year brought a slight revival when, on 1 February 1920, two F2B units were re-formed: No 2 Squadron at Oranmore (OC, Sqn Ldr B. F. Moore) for army co-operation duties with the Irish Command, and No 24 Squadron at Kenley (OC, Sqn Ldr E. H. Johnston) for VIP communications and Air Staff pilot refresher training. On 30 April 1920 a third F2B unit was re-formed at Farnborough, No 4 Squadron (OC, Sqn Ldr C. H. B. Blount, later AVM). It was to be another four years before the next UK-based F2B unit reappeared, when No 13 Squadron (OC, Sqn Ldr C. C. Durston) was re-formed at Kenley on 1 April 1924 from the former Signals Co-operation Flight; and on the same date No 16 Squadron (OC, Sqn Ldr J. O. Archer CBE, later Wg Cdr) re-formed at Old Sarum and was attached to the School of Army

Bottom:
C9837 'B4' of No 12 Squadron RAF — which had previously served as 'C-4' with No 8 Squadron RAF — crashed at Saare, Belgium when Lt Hughes decided to visit No 8 Squadron. *G. Stuart Leslie*

Above left:
A variation in unit markings for this F2B, F4500 of No 2 Squadron RAF.

Left:
F4796, the first F2B delivered to No 106 Squadron RAF at Collingstown, in 1919.
G. Stuart Leslie

Below:
Routine chore. Swinging the compass of F2B F4405.

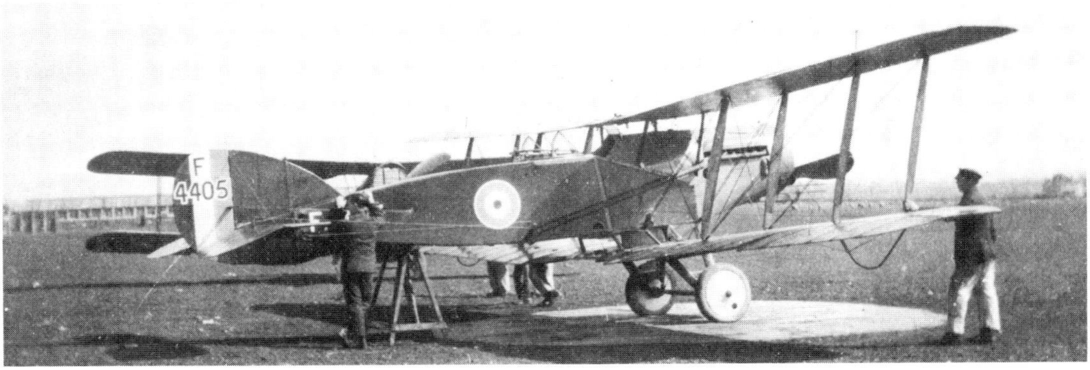

Co-operation at that station. With the exception of No 24 Squadron, all these units were tasked with army co-operation roles, the intended peacetime task for F2Bs in the RAF. For such a role a newly-built F2B, J6586, was widely tested with a range of equipment, including an under fuselage 'pick-up' hook for retrieving messages from the ground — the standard procedure at that time — and provision in the rear cockpit for R/T and W/T signalling equipment if required. Other gear tested was a range of desert-flying items, including a tropical cooling system for eventual operational use in the Middle East and India. Though merely a slightly modified form of the hitherto standard F2B Mk I, J6586 became the 'prototype' for the so-termed 'Mk II' variant, and first of a 215-aircraft batch produced (J6586-J6800) intended primarily for the F2B squadrons based overseas. Until 1922 all F2Bs in RAF service, with few exceptions, remained doped in the standard 1918 colour schemes, but in March 1922 an overall 'aluminium' finish was designated as the future livery and this colouring was generally in use by 1923 throughout the Service squadrons and other units.

In September 1922 one UK-based F2B unit, No 4 Squadron, left Britain embarked on HMS *Ark Royal*, hastily despatched as part of the

Right:
H1420, a Mk III which served with No 4 Squadron RAF for a period, and was then converted to Mk IV standard in September 1928.
C. H. Barnes

Below right:
J8290 of No 13 Squadron RAF wearing one-off markings for a war exercise. *C. H. Barnes*

reinforcements for the British garrison at Chanak, Gallipoli which was facing a possible Turkish 'invasion'. The squadron remained there for a year before returning in September 1923 to Farnborough to resume its normal army co-operation duties. (See chapter 'Middle East 1918-32'.)

Until 1926 most F2Bs had been produced as Mk Is, the wartime production standard, or modified to incorporate the army co-operation and/or overseas roles to become (ostensibly) 'Mk IIs', but in 1926 one F2B, H1420, was modified much further to have a higher load-bearing structure throughout, an oleo tailskid, stronger undercarriage and dual controls. Thoroughly tested in its new form at Old Sarum in the summer of that year, H1420 thus became the prototype F2B Mk III and, after completion of its prototype trials, was then issued to No 4 Squadron for normal service. By the close of the same year, 1926, the RAF had an *overall* strength of approximately 730 first-line aircraft of all types on establishment, spread among 61 squadrons and two Coastal Reconnaissance Flights. Of this total, 12 squadrons — almost 20% of RAF strength — were F2B-equipped; five were in the UK and the rest overseas. In April 1927 another UK unit was sent abroad, when No 2 Squadron sailed aboard HMS *Hermes* to Shanghai as reinforcement for the Shanghai Defence Force during the civil disturbances there, being based on Shanghai Racecourse for these 'operations'. In October 1927, however, No 2 Squadron returned to Manston. In the interim No 13 Squadron at Andover began exchanging its F2Bs for Armstrong Whitworth Atlas aircraft in August 1927. Two years later No 4 Squadron began receiving Atlas aircraft in October 1929, and No 2 Squadron followed suit two months later, leaving No 16 Squadron as the sole F2B squadron in the UK until it too replaced its doughty F2Bs with AW Atlases from January 1931.

Thereafter, the only 'squadron' F2Bs were those flown by the Oxford and Cambridge University Squadrons, each of which was established for five F2Bs in 1930, in addition to their 10 Avro 504N Lynx trainers. These particular F2Bs were modified to Mk IV standard, a further refinement of the Mk III version which incorporated a much strengthened undercarriage and overall structure, automatic Handley Page wing 'slots', and an enlarged fin and horn-balanced rudder. It should be remarked that these F2Bs were among the last F2Bs to bear a newly-introduced RAF colour marking scheme whereby the rudder stripes of red/white/blue were 'reversed' from their former 1918 style; ie from 15 August 1930 all RAF aircraft were ordered to be repainted to display rudder stripes with red next to the rudder hinge-post, and

Below:
J8250 'X', a Mk IV of the Oxford University Air Squadron, in July 1928.

Bottom:
This trio of Oxford UAS's Mk IVs over the Thames Estuary were J8257, 'Z'; J8250, 'X' and J7836, 'Y'. The wing and fuselage band markings were in 'Oxford Blue' colour.
Flight International; ref 10329

Above:
Old warriors never die . . . an F2B serving out its retirement as Instructional Airframe No 213M at No 1 School of Technical Training, Halton, with Aircraft Apprentices being shown the three-man method of 'swinging the prop'. *G. Stuart Leslie*

Below:
One of 12 new-built F2Bs supplied to Spain in 1924 with 300hp Hispano-Suiza engines, oleo undercarriages and Frise ailerons. *C. H. Barnes*

Bottom:
A Type 81A Puma advanced trainer (convertible to a fighter) supplied to the Royal Hellenic Navy, Phaleron Bay, in April 1925. *C. H. Barnes*

the order further required such repainting to be completed on all aircraft by 30 October 1930. These markings supplemented existing authorised Flight distinction colour markings — authorised on 18 December 1924 — whereby wheel cover discs were permitted to be doped Red (A Flight), Yellow (B Flight) or Blue (C Flight) within individual units

By 1932 the Bristol F2B had been generally replaced on all UK-based first-line RAF squadrons, although many individual F2Bs soldiered on as trainers or simply instructional airframes at technical training establishments for several years. At least one F2B achieved 'royal' status in Britain when J8430, the second F2B built of the batch J8429-J8458, was completed in early 1927 and further modified to have HP wing 'slots' and a much-enlarged windscreen added for its rear cockpit. Attached to No 24 Squadron for maintenance purposes, J8430 was the personal transport of Edward, Prince of Wales, later King Edward VIII. F2B F4587, a Mk IV conversion in May 1928, was still flying in 1937, participating in that year's RAF Display at Hendon, and was civil-registered as G-AFHJ in 1938, but was destroyed during World War 2. Today (1985) only two Bristol F2Bs exist in Britain — D8096 of the Shuttleworth Collection (described in chapter 'Civil Sons'), and E2581. The latter machine was first delivered to the RAF on 16 September 1918 and served, mainly, as a hack communication aircraft with various RAF units until its retirement from RAF service in February 1920. It was then earmarked for retention for permanent display at Cardington, and in 1935 was transferred to its present venue, the Imperial War Museum in Lambeth Road, London.

Below:
F2B J8430 was converted for VIP transport, specifically for HRH Edward, Prince of Wales (later HM King Edward VIII), who is seen here climbing into the rear cockpit at Mousehold Heath airfield (the original Norwich Airport) in 1928.

India 1918-32

Although the protracted, turbulent and bloody history of Britain's Imperial control of the sub-continent of India stretched over many years, the major region over which the British air services operated during the years 1916-39 was the North West Frontier Province of India (NWFP), which was 'created' per se by the Viceroy of India, Lord Curzon, on 9 November 1901, and which since 1947 has become West Pakistan. Comprised of specified areas titled Administered and Unadministered Territories, the NWFP came wholly under British rule from 1901 and had a native population overall of some 10 million tribesmen, collectively titled Pathans but comprised of many distinct and individual people with wavering loyalties. Overwhelmingly Moslem by creed, the Pathans were born fighting men whose badge of manhood was the possession of a rifle, however ancient, and an inborn skill as a marksman learned in puberty. As hill and mountain guerilla fighters, these tribesmen had no equals, combining skill, guile, savagery and a computer-like knowledge of their territories which boded ill for any 'invader'. To the Pathan the elation of battle with any non-Moslem 'infidel' was a way of life, and the NWFP became a constant source of dissension, rebellions against the White Raj, escalating often into pitched wars embracing many thousands of men.

During World War 1 the first RFC unit to become based in India was No 31 Squadron, the first personnel of which disembarked in Bombay on 26 December 1915. Remaining in India for the remainder of World War 1, No 31 Squadron gave birth to a second unit, No 114 Squadron at Lahore in September 1917, by providing 114's nucleus of personnel and aircraft. These two squadrons continued to serve in India and Aden after 1918, but the outbreak of the Third Afghan War in May 1919 brought reinforcements in the shapes of Nos 20 and 48 Squadrons, two F2B units based in Germany, both of which reached India by early

Below:

F4611 'D' of 'A' Flight, No 48 Squadron at Quetta, in December 1919. The trisected circle was the unit marking at that period.

Late ACM Sir L. Hollinghurst

June 1919 and were based at Risalpur and Quetta respectively. Almost immediately No 20 Squadron was split into detachments of four F2Bs each at Tank, Bannu and Sora Rogha for operations over the NWFP, with both squadrons flying daily bombing, strafing and general army co-operation sorties. Two more units soon followed to India when No 97 Squadron (DH 10 bombers) arrived from Ford Junction, England in August 1919, and No 99 Squadron DH9As) reached India from Aulnoye, France in the following month. All units became fully committed to repelling the would-be invaders from Afghanistan, one example being the so-termed Battle of Mandanna Hill of 20-25 December 1919 when four F2Bs, six DH9As and three DH10s kept up a constant offensive for the five days' conflict. Such sorties continued into early 1920 and were by no means as one-sided as they might appear to the layman, as exemplified during one raid in the Ahnai Jangi Gorge on 14 January 1920. Three No 20 Squadron F2Bs were lost to accurate Pathan fire, two of these being wrecked and their crews killed while the third crashed but without serious injury to its crew.

Further reinforcement for the RAF came on 20 January 1920 when No 1 Squadron was re-formed (officially) at Risalpur with eventual equipment of single-seat Sopwith Snipe fighters; while at Ambala on 1 February a second Snipe unit, No 3 Squadron, was also re-formed. In the event No 3 was to be disbanded again on 1 October 1921, and No 1 left India for Mesopotamia in April 1922. As these two fighter units re-formed, a curious Air Ministry policy was implemented whereby existing squadrons in India became retitled (despite personal objections from the CAS, Hugh Trenchard). Thus on 1 February 1920 No 48 Squadron now became No 5 Squadron, while No 114 Squadron was renumbered as No 28 Squadron. Then, on 1 April 1920, No 97 Squadron became the reborn No 60 Squadron, and No 99 Squadron became No 27 Squadron. To the crews on the squadrons the new 'labels' made not a jot of difference to their daily routines and operations — or their meagre supply and maintenance situations — and warlike operations continued apace until 7 May, on which date tribal leaders surrendered to terms of 'peace' — a term always relative at *any* period of the NWFP's history.

On 1 June 1920 the RAF in India as a whole could muster a total of only 67 serviceable aircraft of all types — 40 of which were Bristol F2Bs — such was the steadily deteriorating state of maintenance supply and facilities. By September the only unit in direct support of the forward army garrisons in Waziristan was No 20 Squadron. No 20's F2Bs were being maintained in semi-primitive conditions, usually in the open air where they were subject to the constant depredations of a blistering Indian sun, sudden dust and sandstorms, apart from their already ageing engines and airframes. Pilots struggling to maintain or gain altitude in the thin air of the mountainous frontier region suffered constantly from engines overheating, while continuous flying in temperature ranges from zero to 120° Fahrenheit, and navigating through mountain *nullahs* (passes) bounded on all sides by baking rock 'hills' reaching upwards for thousands of feet, meant that the RAF aircrews achieved their skills by dint of undiluted hard experience. Most F2Bs of that era were of 1917-18 vintage — indeed, No 20 Squadron's aircraft still bore patched-over German bullet holes in their fabric-skinned wings — and crews were rapidly reaching the state where they literally took their lives in their own hands each time they took off. One of No 20 Squadron's Flight commanders had his F2B's engine abruptly disintegrate at 2,000ft and only his sheer airmanship skills enabled him to make a safe landing — an incident which very nearly terminated the career of a future Chief of Air Staff, Sir John Slessor.

Under the contemporary arrangements for financing the British fighting services in India, the RAF's annual budget was merely one small section of the main Army account, with an inevitable diminution of the RAF's allotment of monies. As one ex-F2B pilot put it: 'We flew over the Frontier hills on one magneto because the government of India could "not afford" to pay for a second . . .'.

Left:
H1518 'P' of No 5 Squadron high over the Quetta region, close to the Baluchistan mountains, in 1922.

In India in 1920-21 it was no uncommon practice for three or even four aircraft to be cannibalised for 'spare' parts in order to put one serviceable aircraft into the air. Even then F2Bs were often forced to embark on operations, with full war loads, on their bare metal wheel rims — new tyres were 'unavailable' when requested from depot stores. It was a state of affairs which was to last for several years, and was only partially resolved by the protests of several individuals; one of whom was the commander of No 31 Squadron — which had re-equipped with F2Bs in early 1920 — Sqn Ldr Arthur Harris AFC (later MRAF Sir Arthur Harris GCB, OBE, AFC, LLD), whose summary of conditions was:

'We lacked practically everything which an air force squadron anywhere else would regard as essential for maintaining its aircraft. We came under the Army Vote and, as a result, we got little of everything and much of what we got was useless as, for instance, the photographic materials and chemicals, which had all deteriorated until they were no good. We had single-ignition Rolls-Royce Falcon engines (dependent on one contact breaker) when new dual-ignition engines were being sold for a song as surplus in England!'

The overall effect of this deplorable situation was reflected in the annual average figures for flying hours accomplished. Throughout 1921 each aircraft in India was deemed to have flown a scanty average of 44 hours, compared with, for example, 119 hours per aircraft (average) stationed with the RAF in Iraq.

Serviceability continued to depreciate during 1922 although this did not deter the aircrews from trying their utmost to fulfil their duties. On 6 April four squadrons were ordered to muster 'all available' aircraft for immediate operations against a large tribal force investing the army garrison at Wana Fort. Of 30 aircraft ostensibly available in those squadrons only 12 could be accurately termed as serviceable, seven of these being F2Bs. By the end of the same month of the six resident squadrons in India (No 1 Squadron had embarked for Iraq on 27 April 1922), only 49 aircraft were declared fit for operations, 38 of which were Bristol F2Bs. This meagre total was expected to maintain constant and ever-ready support for all forward army garrisons and other formations scattered widely throughout a land area of almost 30,000 square miles — roughly the size of Scotland. Full establishment (on paper) for a Bristol F2B squadron at that time comprised 12

Facing page, top:
'A' Flight, No 5 Squadron lined up at Quetta in 1922. From nearest, H1530, 'A'; F4403, 'C'; and an unidentified F2B.

Facing page, bottom:
H1554 of No 28 Squadron, in 1923, with well sun-blistered fabric.

Left:
F4320 'D' of No 31 Squadron over Lahore in 1923. By 1927 this F2B was 'D' of 'A' Flight, No 5 Squadron.

Below:
Tucking in close. F4839 of No 31 Squadron — pilot, Flg Off Fresson, with air gunner, LAC France — during a close formation flight over Delhi. Note that the spare wheel was stowed *under* the fuselage below the rear cockpit.
No 31 Squadron Association

Above:
Flg Off Ford in J6782 of No 32 Squadron, taking-off from Dardoni, North West Frontier Province in 1923.

Right:
J6750, the aircraft of No 5 Squadron's 'C' Flight commander, c1924.

Below right:
E2421 'C' of No 5 Squadron en route from Tank to Jelal Khel during 'Pink's War' in 1925.

aircraft, 21 officers, 25 NCOs, 89 airmen and 90 Indian tradesmen and labourers. Yet on 31 August 1922, of the four F2B units, only 27 of the 48-aircraft establishment were in any manner fit for flying. And those four units — Nos 5, 20, 28 and 31 Squadrons — represented two-thirds of the RAF's fighting potential throughout India. The scandal — for it was no less — of the RAF's position in India brought insistent pressure upon the British government to take immediate action, and accordingly AVM Sir John Salmond was sent out to India to investigate and report on the whole situation. Salmond's findings were summarised succinctly in a 37-page report to the Viceroy of India in August 1922. In precise, reasoned yet blunt terms, Salmond declared the RAF in India as being virtually ineffective in its existing state, and whose subordination to the Army *had* to be rectified promptly if air control was to be exploited fully. Among his many recommendations was the raising of the squadron establishment from six to eight. Although his report and recommendations were agreed by higher authority, it should be remarked that it was to be a further six years before the two extra squadrons actually arrived in India.

While Salmond's arrival created a stir among Service and civil hierarchy in India, leading to a hasty but still totally inadequate trickle of long-awaited spares from depots and stores to the squadrons, operations continued with the existing meagre resources. On 17 December 1922 these operations intensified in the Razmak area and No 28 Squadron moved from Kohat to the forward 'airfield' at Fort Dardoni. In the freezing winter conditions operations continued daily until May 1923. Between the six squadrons a total of 56 aircraft were available on 31 December 1922, of which 38 were Bristol F2Bs. On 24 January 1923 six F2Bs from No 28 Squadron set out to bomb villages on the south side of Bakri Punga, each loaded with a dozen 20/25lb Cooper bombs and carrying three boxes of Baby Incendiaries. One of these F2Bs, piloted by Flg Off R. M. Foster DFC (later ACM Sir Robert Foster KCB, CBE, DFC), with his observer, Flg Off L. H. Ridley, began attacking its target but broke away abrupty when the bottom fell out of one box of incendiaries and several ignited. Ridley quickly threw out some of the burning incendiaries, being badly burned in the process, but one incendiary had rolled under the rear petrol tank. Foster put his F2B down as fast as possible, force-landing in a rocky valley and turning the aircraft over in the process. Both men escaped injury in the crash and promptly got away from the wreck which erupted in flames, then exploded within minutes. Twenty minutes later both men were caught by Manzir Khan tribesmen, immediately beaten up and had most of their clothing taken, then were taken to separate villages where they were tied up by night and placed in the open centre of villages by day as a deterrent to further bombing by RAF aircraft (with the threat of being shot if any bomb fell). Their incarceration lasted until their final release on 12 February, unharmed.

Apart from all the common hazards of flying over mountainous territory, and the various possibilities of physical torture or death at the hands of tribesmen in the event of capture, the RAF crews also faced dangers from constantly varying weather conditions. In July 1923, for merely one example, during a series of sporadic raids near Razmak, dense clouds suddenly closed in among the hills surrounding the target area and caused several crashes, including two F2Bs of No 20 Squadron whose four crew members were killed. Such problems were accepted as almost a matter of routine by the RAF crews, and operations continued unabated, despite continuing poor serviceability generally among the squadrons due to the paucity of maintenance supply still.

In 1925 however the six RAF squadrons in India were given a unique opportunity to demonstrate the efficacy of air power alone in dealing with

Above:

C801 'A' of No 5 Squadron being piloted by Flt Lt A. C. Sanderson DFC in 1927. Sanderson later rose to become Air Marshal Sir Clifford KBE, CB, DFC before retiring from the RAF in 1955. *C. H. Barnes*

tribal uprisings. From July to October 1924 tribes in southern Waziristan, notably the Mahsuds, had engaged in a number of attacks on government and Service outposts but had finally been subjugated and came to terms with one exception, the Abdur Rahman Khel, a tribe which continued its forays against army posts at Manzai, Gomal and Spli Toi. The AOC, RAF India therefore decided to mount conclusive air operations against these stubborn rebels — but *without* the hitherto customary support of costly and cumbrous army formations. To command the whole operation Wg Cdr R. C. M. Pink, OC No 2 (India) Wing, was nominated, and he made his headquarters for this at the old fort at Tank (pronounced 'Tonk').

On 3 March 1925 two flights from each of Nos 27 and 60 Squadrons — totalling 16 DH9s — flew to the Tochi Scout HQ at Miramshah, being the first squadrons to actually occupy this Fort, though RAF aircraft had utilised it as an emergency landing field for several years. Four days later they were joined by the remaining Flights of each unit. Meanwhile Pink had moved to Tank where No 5 Squadron became based with its 10 Bristol F2Bs. On 9 March operations commenced with raids on all sections of the tribes, usually in the form of day bombing by the DH9s with 112lb and 230lb bombs on villages, co-ordinated with machine gun strafing sweeps by the Bristols against neighbouring caves and hill refuges. These were customarily flown at 3,000ft above the targets — the primary target being up to 6,000ft above sea level and thus necessitating only partial bomb loads to ensure that bombers could attain a safe altitude over the mountainous terrain. The initial attacks set fire to several villages and a watch tower was destroyed, resulting in promises from some tribal sections to comply with the government's demands, and therefore a temporary cessation of bombing on 13 March. Since nothing came of those promises, however, operations began again on 14 March, and three days later the whole Abdur Rahman Khel tribe arrived at Jandola for a *jirga* (meeting) with government representatives. Discussions at the *jirga* broke down and operations continued, while on 18 March one Flight of No 20 Squadron's F2Bs was moved up to Tank to reinforce No 5 Squadron.

Three days later, on 21 March, occurred the only RAF casualties of the whole campaign when a No 27 Squadron DH9A was shot down by rifle-fire and exploded into the ground, killing the two-man crew. By the end of March operations reached a peak of activity, with normal bombing and strafing sorties being interspersed with blockade patrols on which pairs of aircraft with two 112lb and eight 20/25lb bombs apiece were despatched at irregular intervals during daylight hours to keep the tribesmen 'unsettled'. These nuisance raids were supplemented by W/T patrols on wide sweeps which signalled back to base on sighting any tribal movement for aircraft already on 5-10-minute readiness to be sent direct to any designated area. These tactics were further supplemented on 30 March when a single F2B from No 31 Squadron was flown from the squadron base at Ambala to Tank for a planned night foray. Until then all tribesmen had considered themselves immune from bombing after sundown, but on the night of 4 April the No 31 Squadron F2B shattered that illusion most emphatically, in particular by killing one notorious Faridai leader, Tormarchai, in the proceedings. This success led to two more F2Bs being flown up to Tank on 6 April, followed immediately by the rest of No 31 Squadron becoming based at Tank, while No 5 Squadron's F2Bs were detached to Miramshah along with a Flight of F2Bs of No 20 Squadron, and the DH9As of Nos 27 and 60 Squadrons.

Operations continued at an intense pace by day and by night until finally, on 28 April, representatives of all rebelling tribes met government officials at Jandola to begin three days of talks ending on 1 May with agreed terms, on which date all operations ceased. During the 54 days of actual operations the RAF crews had flown a total of 2,720 hours, and all personnel of No 2 (India) Wing became eligible for what is probably the rarest British campaign medal ever issued, the India General Service Medal 1908, in silver, with a

Above:
Busy scene as No 20 Squadron's F2Bs rev up for a squadron patrol in 1929.

Right:
J6752 'K' of No 20 Squadron.

clasp 'Waziristan 1925', for which a total of only 46 officers and 214 non-commissioned airmen were qualified. Wg Cdr Pink, the unorthodox and universally respected commander of this 'mini-war' received not only accelerated promotion to Group Captain but a form of 'immortality' in RAF annals by having the operations thereafter referred to by all concerned as 'Pink's War'. His own typical reaction to the event was well summarised in a fragment of rhyme he had composed during his many flights during the operations, entitled *Waziristan 1925*, part of which reads:

Above left:
F4463, which served with Nos 5, 31 and 20 Squadrons until 1930, is seen here on air test after a major overhaul at the Aircraft Depot at Drigh Road, Karachi, with LAC Hambrook occupying the rear cockpit. *MoD (Air); H833*

Left:
E2605 'C' of No 28 Squadron makes a three-point landing. . . . This F2B also served with No 20 Squadron. *Via R. C. B. Ashworth*

Above:
H1461 'F' and H1457 'E' of No 31 Squadron leaving Peshawar in 1930, with underwing panniers loaded and other personal crew gear stowed under the fuselages. H1461 had previously flown with No 5 Squadron in 1926.
31 Squadron Association

'Oh smart Brisfit, oh smart Brisfit
What are you doing in fighting kit?
I'm praying hard I'll avoid a konk
On offensive patrols from a sink called Tank.

Chorus
'Up the gorges and down Spli Toi
Sniped to blazes but attaboy
They call it war on the banks of the Marne
But bless you it's *peace* in Waziristan.
Don't you worry, there's nought to tell
'Cept work and fly and bomb like hell
With hills above us and hills below
And rocks to fill where the hills won't go
Nice soft sitting for those who crash
But WAR you call it? — don't talk trash
War's a rumour, war's a yarn
This is the PEACE of Waziristan.'

In November 1925 Pink returned to England, but on 7 March 1932, just after his promotion to Air Commodore, he died in hospital at RAF Halton of cancer — a tragic loss of a brilliant officer and leader of men.

The legacy of Pink's outstanding abilities could fairly be said to be the change — albeit a grudging one — in the Army and civil hierarchy's attitude thereafter to the potential of air power in India, particularly in the context of air control and containment of rebel tribal forces. By 1926 this change in views was reflected in a great improvement in general maintenance of the RAF's aircraft and other equipment and facilities. For example, No 5 Squadron's F2Bs flew an annual total of 3,194 hours that year; an average of 266 hours per F2B. Although anti-tribal operations continued spasmodically much of the Bristol F2Bs' work was flown in their major role of army co-operation. These duties comprised many hours of photo-reconnaissance to enable accurate mapping of the overall territory, and constant seeking of an improvement in direct air-ground-air communications with outlying and mobile army formations. All F2Bs were fitted with the standard under-fuselage pick-up hook for retrieving messages from the ground, but a major problem was the development of a satisfactory means of delivering such intelligence to army columns out among the hills and mountains. To fly low over would-be recipients and hand-drop message bags was not only time-wasting but decidedly dangerous for the aircrews fighting to maintain control of their aircraft in the up-currents and heat 'bumping' among the bare mountains.

In 1927 a series of experiments were made with the use of W/T and R/T equipment fitted into the rear cockpits of Bristol F2Bs, but while W/T, using the Morse code, was reasonably successful, the R/T procedures produced poor results in the main. Apart from any technical difficulties — the F2B airframe was never satisfactory for safe bonding — the gunners found the contemporary R/T sets bulky and cumbersome. On 21 February 1927, at a mass demonstration of the RAF held at Delhi, F2Bs gave a successful example of R/T procedures both in the air and in an air-ground-air set-up, but generally speaking it was considered more efficient to have each squadron set aside one or two F2Bs specifically fitted out for R/T tasks. The duties of F2B back-seat crewmen were well described by Air Cdre Tyndall-Carill-Worsley who served as a junior officer-pilot with No 20 Squadron over the NWFP at that time:

Right:
Indian postings were hot, but freezing at altitude. This is LAC Wright of No 5 Squadron, Quetta in 1922, fully booted and spurred for a flight.

Left:
A No 28 Squadron F2B at Secunderabad on 17 January 1931. Note the desert tyres and extra coolant outlet.
Courtesy OC No 28 Squadron R-RAF

'In the Bristol Fighters and (later) Westland Wapitis which we flew, the Lewis guns were on Scarff mountings and consequently, particularly in the Brisfit (F2B), the aircraftman in the back seat was particularly uncomfortable and had many long, boring, monotonous hours on reconnaissance flights, just hoping the pilot might have a message to pass which would at least break the tedium and keep him in practice. The accepted method of passing the time was to play noughts-and-crosses by wireless with the duty operator back at squadron headquarters.

'This was carried on in a sort of W/T shorthand code which all wireless-operators knew, but which few pilots could ever understand. On one of my first flights, at the end of a long artillery-spotting exercise, I was mystified to be handed a chit from the rear cockpit which was a message from base, consisting entirely of four letters, "PUFO". It had to be explained to me that this was the traditional way for base to pass permission to return, and was simply an abbreviation for "Pack Up and —— OFF!". In between times, when one had permission to bomb, the poor air gunner just had to sit there and take it whilst one went through all the violent manoeuvres involved in a good beat-up. One occupational hazard for pilots in those times, especially new ones, was the danger of getting a good wallop on the head from the Lewis gun as the gunner decided to move it from side to side, via a forward arc instead of towards the rear. When doing high-level, as opposed to dive-bombing, the air gunner did the bomb-aiming, using the High Altitude Drift Sight clamped alongside the fuselage. To do this he had to lean over the side and, since there was no intercom, he "requested" alterations of course by reaching over and thumping the pilot on the appropriate shoulder.'

It should be added here that at the period in question only two official categories of full-time aircrew existed in the RAF, ie pilot and Observer. The vast bulk of air gunners were in fact volunteer ground tradesmen eager to fly. The job carried no advancement in promotion, but financially such gunners could be awarded an extra sixpence per day if 'regularly' engaged on such duties, plus a further 18 pence per day added to their meagre pay '. . . when employed on operations'.

By June 1927 full operations were in progress again in the Beshawar district, where the F2Bs of Nos 5 and 20 Squadrons joined with the DH9As of Nos 27 and 60 Squadrons in helping to repel a large tribal force intent on investing Peshawar. Again, No 5 Squadron's F2Bs undertook a night-bombing role to good effect, using the technique of bombing by the light of airburst flares. These particular operations were relatively brief, but were noteworthy in one respect in that one of the minor rebel tribal leaders was one Mirza Ali Khan — later to become notorious as the Faqir of Ipi and a constant thorn in the sides of the Indian and British governmental authorities for many years to come.

In December 1928 two new squadrons, Nos 11 and 39, arrived in India — the long-promised extra units recommended by AVM Salmond's 1922 report — and both were equipped with Westland Wapiti aircraft. In the same month came the first general issue of parachutes to all aircrews in India — an 'innovation' not entirely welcomed by many of the more experienced pilots who regarded the Irvin 'chutes as an 'unnecessary encumbrance' in their cockpits, though the carriage of same was soon made mandatory by Air Ministry order. Prior to the arrival of the new squadrons, a general reorganisation of the RAF in India was implemented whereby after October 1928 the

RAF strength was disposed:

Group HQ, Peshawar	No 20 Squadron (F2B)
No 1 (India) Wing	
Kohat	No 27 Squadron (DH9A)
	No 60 Squadron (DH9A)
No 2 (India) Wing	
Risalpur	No 11 Squadron (Wapiti IIA)
	No 39 Squadron (Wapiti IIA)
No 3 (India) Wing	
Quetta	No 5 Squadron (F2B)
	No 31 Squadron (F2B)
Air HQ, Ambala	No 28 Squadron (F2B)
Lahore	Aircraft Park
Drigh Road, Karachi	Aircraft Depot

The years 1929 and 1930 proved as turbulent as most along the North West Frontier Province and the Afghan border territories, with the prime kernel of dissension being instigated in 1929 by the Indian National Congress party — inspired by Mahatma Ghandi — organising a massive civil disobedience movement. This rebellion was assisted by one Abdul Ghaffar Khan of Utmanzai who organised the Frontier Youth League which adopted red uniforms for its members, giving rise to the more common title of 'Red Shirts'. These 'Red Shirts' were to be at the centre of numerous uprisings over the following years. Yet again the ageing Bristol F2Bs were brought into first-line operational use as bombers and strafers. Bomb loads usually comprised eight or 12 20/25lb Cooper bombs, weapons highly under-rated by army commanders until the occasion when one Cooper bomb was dropped on the Peshawar Bombing Range and killed or injured 17 Indian cavalrymen who had strayed in error on to the target area. Nevertheless, these 'Red Shirt' campaigns were to be the Bristol F2Bs' final major operations in India, because in 1931 came their gradual replacement on the squadrons by Westland Wapitis. No 5 Squadron commenced re-equipment with Wapitis in February 1931 and completed the process by May; then No 28 Squadron began exchanging its well-worn F2Bs in September; while No 31 Squadron received its first Wapiti on 13 February 1931 and had been fully converted from F2Bs by 16 April. These changes left only No 20 Squadron still soldiering on with F2Bs temporarily, but in January 1932 Wapitis began arriving on the unit and re-equipment was completed by April that year, thereby making No 20 Squadron the longest-serving F2B unit in the RAF, having flown the type — virtually unchanged from its original design — for nearly 15 years.

Below:
Swan song. The last formation flight of No 20 Squadron, leaving Peshawar on 13 March 1932.

Middle East 1918-32

In the Middle East, at the moment of the November 1918 Armistice, only two units were fully equipped with Bristol F2Bs, the Australian No 1 Squadron AFC, and No 139 Squadron RAF. The Australian unit, renumbered from No 67 Squadron RFC on 6 February 1918, was based at Ramleh, Palestine on that date but moved to Kantara, Egypt in February 1919, having handed over 12 Bristol F2Bs to No 111 Squadron RAF at Ramleh, which had just been reconstituted as a fighter-reconnaissance unit. With its 'A' and 'B' flights detached to Aleppo and Damascus in Syria respectively from March 1919 to oversee local unrest, No 111 Squadron began re-equipping with Sopwith Snipe fighters at the end of that year, but on 1 February 1920 was effectively disbanded by being renumbered No 14 Squadron. No 139 Squadron, based at Arcade, four miles south of the Piave River in Italy, since 1 November 1918, was also disbanded quickly, on 7 March 1919. However, the contemporary Air Ministry policy of changing unit labels around gave rebirth to a famous wartime unit, No 208 Squadron when, on 1 February 1920, No 113 Squadron based at Ismailia, Egypt was renumbered. On that date the new 208 was equipped with RE8s, but by October it began receiving Bristol F2Bs in their place.

The overall task facing the RAF in the Middle East following World War 1 was a prodigious one. In addition to her normal responsibilities for overseas member-countries of the (then) British

Below:
A No 4 Squadron F2B taking-off from HMS *Argus* on 11 October 1922.

Empire, Britain had inherited large areas of the Near and Middle East as mandated territories and was therefore responsible for administration, control and development of such territories until their ultimate self-assertion as independent states. Resulting from the Trenchard/Churchill Memorandum of December 1919, which outlined a proposed basis for the future of the RAF, the bulk of RAF squadrons were to be based overseas, and as a key 'halfway house' between Great Britain and her eastern Empire, Egypt was considered most suitable as the location for central control of all RAF units in the Mediterranean zones, in addition to the contemporary vital necessity for Britain to protect the Suez Canel route to the Far East. The major area under Britain's mandatory control was Mesopotamia — 'Mespot' to the British Servicemen — which was at that time a loosely defined territory including much of the later Iraq and Iran (Persia). For air control of this mandate the Cairo Conference of March 1921 concluded that eight squadrons would be required. By then Nos 6, 8, 30, 55 and 84 Squadrons were already based around the area and therefore No 1 Squadron (Sopwith Snipes) was transferred from India, and Nos 45 and 70 Squadrons were transferred from their Egyptian bases in 1922.

Of these eight units No 6 Squadron was the only F2B unit. At the close of World War 1, No 6 had been an RE8 army co-operation unit, and arrived initially at Basra on 18 July 1919. Based at Mosul the squadron began receiving Bristol F2Bs by July 1920 and almost immediately became embroiled in operations against a widespread anti-British revolt led by the notorious Sheikh Mahmoud. This sheikh was an idealistic fanatic who, since 1915, had pursued a constant denial of foreign control of Kurdistan — a nebulous area covering northern Mesopotamia, western Persia, parts of southern Russia and the old Ottoman or Turkish Empire. Mahmoud was to become the leading dissident in the area over the following 10 years, and his constant attempts to bring about a united Kurdistan (under his personal rule) earned him the ironic 'title' of 'C-in-C, RAF Training' from his RAF adversaries. All RAF units became involved in quelling this 1920 rebellion, with No 6 Squadron flying a total of 210 hours, dropping 1,661lb of bombs and firing 3,730 rounds of ammunition on operations in June alone.

Nevertheless, the larger menace to peace in Mesopotamia then was the growing ambitions of Turkey to the north. After her humiliating defeat by the Allied Powers in 1918, Turkey under the vital leadership of Mustafa Kemal had quickly emerged as a new, energetic nation, hungry to reclaim her lands 'lost' by the 1918 Armistice terms. By first instigating unrest among Kurdish tribes, particularly in the vilayet of Mosul, Turkey rapidly spread her tentacles south and westwards. On 26 August 1922 the Turks heavily defeated a Greek army at Anatolia and pursued its remnants to Smyrna, which was promptly invested and sacked. Continuing their triumphant march to Constantinople, the Turks arrived there in mid-September and encamped on the borders of the Gallipoli 'neutral' zone near Chanak. Here they came into direct opposition to the British military occupation force based in the area. This overt threat to international peace brought swift countermeasures by the RAF with the despatch of three squadrons (Nos 4, 25 and 207) from Britain, while from Egypt came No 208 Squadron's Bristol F2Bs and a Flight from No 56 Squadron, later joined by a Flight from Malta-based No 267 Squadron — all these units now titled Constantinople Wing, RAF. No 4 Squadron's F2Bs were embarked on HMS *Ark Royal* and arrived in Kilia Bay on 8 October, being transferred to HMS *Argus* three days later. On 11 October No 4 Squadron took off from *Argus* — the first time any of the F2B pilots had ever flown off an aircraft carrier — and all arrived on Kilia airfield without incident. Their companion F2B unit, No 208 Squadron, took up residence at San Stefano airfield from 28 September 1922, having been embarked on SS *Podesta* on 25 September with its F2Bs dismantled in crates.

Assembly of the Bristols at San Stefano was accomplished relatively quickly and 208's first operational flights were made on 5 October. Throughout October No 208 Squadron became busy with daily reconnaissance sorties, keeping the British cavalry commanders updated on the disposition of Turkish troops, interspersed with practice bomb-dropping, general artillery co-operation and W/T work. Like No 208 Squadron, the F2B crews of No 4 Squadron attempted manfully to provide tactical and strategic support for the army formations, but were steadily frustrated by the encroaching winter conditions. In its first two weeks No 4 had experienced violent dust-storms and extreme heat conditions, but with the advent of the rain season its airfield rapidly deteriorated into a quagmire, on which the F2Bs could not take-off, land or even taxi, often sinking axle-deep in the glutinous mud. Then, towards the end of October 1922, 60-70mph gales added to the unit's misery, blowing down and wrecking hangars and tented accommodation, followed by rains which brought extensive flooding of the area. One of the few 'light' moments of this demoralising period came when one of the portable canvas hangars issued from storage to the unit on its move from the UK was unpacked and unrolled prior to initial assembly. Inside were some letters and parcels, dated 1916, with one letter signed by 'Two Old Ladies of Ascot'! One scheme attempting to

Above:
The original F2B D8096, with No 208 Squadron at San Stefano, Turkey. Its serial is today (1985) carried by the sole surviving flying F2B which is with the Shuttleworth Collection at Old Warden, Bedfordshire. *G. Stuart Leslie*

Below:
High stuff. C823 (leading), E2529 (right) and F4580 (far centre) of No 6 Squadron over Baibu, Kurdistan — the mountain Gara Dagh in background is 11,500ft high. These three F2Bs had served previously with Nos 141, 3 AFC and 138 Squadrons respectively.

Bottom:
F4435 of No 208 Squadron over Ismailia, Egypt in 1925.

Above:
No 208 Squadron's F2Bs 'on parade'.

Below:
F2Bs H1492 (nearest) and J6685 of No 208 Squadron on 24 March 1924, with Sgt W. Lawrence (left) and Flg Off Millen in attendance. The black 'Club' was 'A' Flight's marking and appeared on the fin, upper centre-section and under the starboard lower wing.

Bottom:
'Shiny Six' — No 6 Squadron — undergoing the annual ritual of AOC's Inspection by AVM Sir Robert Brooke-Popham KCB, at Mosul in 1928. The unit got its nickname for its passion for highly polishing all metal fittings (engine cowlings et al). Note that all propellers are *exactly* horizontal — checked by plumb-line!
Courtesy OC, No 6 Squadron RAF

resolve the liquid mud problem involved constructing a rough runway measuring 60yd by 10yd of wire netting stretched over canvas and pegged down. Even this remedy was only partially successful — on this runway F2Bs still sank up to 6in. By January 1923 the squadron gave up the unequal struggle and moved en bloc to Kilid el Bahr instead, where all aircraft were maintained wholly in the open, there being no hangars available by then.

The RAF Constantinople Wing remained at readiness in the area for the first eight months of 1923, ie until a 'peace' treaty was ratified in Lausanne on 23 August 1923, during which time all squadrons continued their prime role of co-operation with the army. During the month of April, apart from such routine duties, No 208 Squadron's F2Bs flew a reasonably large number of sorties in liaison with the local Royal Navy force, including a few novel experiments. One example came on 10 April when a Bristol F2B circled HMS *Seraphis* off Proti Island in the Marmora Sea. The exercise was to test the feasibility of an aircraft bombing a torpedo when this was launched — without prior warning — from a naval vessel. At 10.25hrs a torpedo was fired, set for an 8,000yd run at a depth of 18ft. When this was approximately 3,000yd from the ship the F2B dropped a single 112lb bomb from 150ft height which entered the water ahead and slight left of the torpedo. The bomb exploded two seconds later as the torpedo passed, the torpedo surfaced 20yd farther on, stopped, veered 45deg to port, then continued slowly running with leaking oil slick, smoke and intermittent flaring — a clear tribute to the F2B crew's bombing skill. With the ratification of 'peace' on 23 August, orders were given the following day to evacuate the units of the Constantinople Wing from the area, and in the first week of September No 208 Squadron was shipped in SS *Winnow* and SS *Khartoum* to Alexandria and eventually 'set up shop' again at Ismailia, its former base; in the same month No 4 Squadron returned to England and its old base at Farnborough.

Before this Turkish threat to peace in the Middle East — usually referred to in history books as the Chanak Incident — the RAF had other heavy responsibilities placed upon its shoulders. In September 1921 Mesopotamia was renamed Iraq and on 1 October 1922, in accord with the provisions of the Cairo Conference, the newly-titled mandate was placed under overall RAF control, with its first AOC, Air Vice-Marshal Sir John Salmond, taking up his appointment officially from 22 October. Salmond had hardly settled in before he was faced with a serious threat to peace, when the recalcitrant Sheikh Mahmoud calmly declared himself as 'King of Kurdistan' and announced a *jehad* (holy war) against the British occupation forces. Salmond immediately concentrated a total of 42 aircraft drawn from Nos 6, 8, 30 and 45 Squadrons and launched air operations against Mahmoud, paying particular attention to Sulamaniya, the city where Mahmoud had made his 'palace' and headquarters. This promptly received a total of 28 tons of bombs during operations which eventually dragged on into 1924, but in July 1924 British and Iraqi troops occupied Sulamaniya and Mahmoud's activities were — at least temporarily — nullified. Almost immediately the scene of operations shifted back to the Mosul district where Turkey renewed her attempts to occupy the Mosul vilayet. On 13 September 1924 intelligence was received that Turks intended crossing the frontier to seize Zakho that same night. Nine F2Bs from No 6 Squadron took off at dawn on 14 September and within 15 minutes had discovered some 300 Turkish cavalry crossing the River Borana. Sweeping into action the Bristol crews swiftly dispersed these troops at the cost of one pilot wounded by ground fire. Refuelled and re-armed, the F2Bs returned and effectively strafed and bombed a second Turkish cavalry formation of some 150 horsemen at Birkar. This highly effective and immediate retaliation became a pattern for stultifying subsequent occasional forays by Turkey into Iraq, until an eventual League of Nations initiative resulted in a tripartite peace agreement in 1926 at Angora.

In 1924 too trouble erupted in Palestine when a force of 4,000 of Ibn Saud's fanatical Wahabi followers began plundering. On 14 August No 14 Squadron's mixture of Bristol F2Bs and recently-arrived DH9As, supporting a formation of RAF armoured cars, dispersed the main force of Wahabis in the Ziza Plain, 12 miles south of Amman. No 14 Squadron, which had inherited its F2Bs from the renumbered No 111 Squadron in 1920 at Ramleh, was to continue using a mixture of F2Bs and DH9As until 1926 when it became fully established as a DH9A bomber unit. Meanwhile Sheikh Mahmoud resumed his attempts to oust the British from his self-declared 'kingdom' in the spring of 1925. No 6 Squadron's F2Bs combined with the DH9As of No 30 and 55 Squadrons, and a Flight of No 1 Squadron's Sopwith Snipes, to subdue this latest outbreak of hostilities. On 20 June Mahmoud gathered as many of his followers as possible for an all-out attack on Choarta but was defeated and he fled to Persia. A year later Mahmoud returned from his refuge to stir up dissension, only to be defeated quickly by prompt air action in which No 6 Squadron figured prominently, leaving Mahmoud to retreat to his Persian bolt-hole yet again. Undeterred, however, Mahmoud made another attempt in June 1926 and fighting on the ground soon reached a critical stage for British and Iraqi forces, but intensive air action on 17-19 June turned the odds in favour of the government troops and Mahmoud once more fled to Persia. Within the following months Mahmoud was persuaded to visit Baghdad for talks with government representatives and eventually agreed to terms, and for the next three years he remained inactive.

With Mahmoud's constant activities muted, a decision was taken to strengthen government forces in another rebel leader's area of influence in 1927, when simmering unrest among the tribes in central Kurdistan was being engendered by Sheikh Ahmad of Barzan. Ahmad had been hostile to foreign administration since 1919 and stepped up his covert opposition from 1925 when the area over which he wielded power came under the nominal administration of the Iraq government. Thus in 1927 a force of Iraq Levies, supported by No 6 Squadron and a Flight of No 55 Squadron's DH9As, occupied Barzan, and this move caused Ahmad and his 'court' to flee to the hills. No 6 Squadron, at this period the only Bristol F2B unit based in Iraq, in many ways held a unique position. As with most RAF squadrons outside Britain, it was in most respects virtually an independent formation, near self-contained, with its commanding officer being almost solely responsible for maintaining peace (in the context of all aerial activities) in a land area almost as big as England — and with just 12 aircraft. Based at Mosul, No 6 Squadron received a new commander in January 1928, Sqn Ldr C. H. Keith (later Group Captain), whose first impression of his new command was:

'My command is within a barbed wire perimeter camp — with the exception of the water-pumping and purifying station and the ice plant, which are as near as possible on the right bank of the Tigris. The place is intended to be defensible, and I am supposed to have, within the barbed wire, all the necessities of life to hold out, if surrounded. There is a complete army co-operation squadron (No 6) of Bristol Fighter aircraft, No 8 Section of our Armoured Car Company, a Supply Depot, a wireless station and a sort of small hospital. . . . The job, as a job, is a good one, and I am almighty glad to get it. It is probably the most independent Squadron Leader's command in the entire RAF.' (*Flying Years*, by C. H. Keith; J. Hamilton, 1937.)

Despite the myriad dangers of flying and active operations over such a vast bald desert and its attendant towering hills, there was a quality to the experiences gained by No 6 Squadron's F2B crews which is unlikely ever to be known again by modern aircrews. As one ex-No 6 Squadron pilot has, almost poetically, described his feelings:

'Flying over the Kurdistan mountains was an experience which rarely lost its fearful charm . . . gazing down on row after row of misty white peaks, looking like sleeping giants; deep, dark

Below:
FR4582 of No 208 Squadron — a locally rebuilt machine, hence the *FR* serial prefix.
Via R. C. B. Ashworth

valleys whose sides are so sheer that one wonders that even light cares to penetrate into their depths.'

For all such delights in the wonders of raw nature, flying above Iraq also brought out the darker facets. In summer the airfield would bake in temperatures of 120° plus in the *shade*, and once airborne a pilot had to overcome heat 'bumps' capable of knocking the control column violently out of his grasp and plunging an aircraft down for a thousand feet or more before he could regain control. Operations in a Bristol F2B among the mountains of Kurdistan called for ingrained experience and skill. To attack a rebel native village or camp in the valleys between cliff-faces reaching thousands of feet to the sky meant diving at a speed high enough to 'bounce' the aircraft high enough on pull-out to climb over the nearby mountain face, and too often only the excellence of an F2B's Rolls-Royce Falcon engine stood between death or survival. As another ex-No 6 Squadron pilot summed up his experience in the late 1920s: 'I learned more about handling aircraft — and my own limitations — in 18 months on "Shiny Six" than in 10 years of Service flying in England.'

On 1 October 1929 No 6 Squadron sent off the first party of one officer and 25 airmen in five Victoria transport aircraft of No 70 Squadron, bound eventually for Moascar, Ismailia in Egypt; the start of a complete squadron move of base by air, land and rail which brought to a close the squadron's 10 years of service in Iraq. Before leaving Mosul some squadron airmen carved out the unit's badge and motto on a huge rockface at Abu Saif, just south of the airfield, as a 'memorial' to the squadron's service there. The squadron's move was of particular interest to the Air Staff as an experiment in transferring an entire squadron including all personnel and equipment from one Command to another, and to arrive at its destination able to be employed on normal duties without delay. The land distance from Mosul to Moascar was slightly over 1,000 miles, all across deserts, routeing via Shergat, Baiji, Baghdad, Rutbah, Amman, Jerusalem and across the Sinai to the Suez Canal. It meant moving 12 aircraft (and crews), 12 officers, 114 airmen and sufficient supplies in 24 Crossley Tenders by road and air, and this was eventually accomplished without mishap by 11 November; the dozen Bristol F2Bs left Mosul by air on 2 November and arrived at Moascar two days later. The readiness of No 6 Squadron was soon tested when, on 18 November, 'A' Flight was detached to Ramleh, Palestine where it was joined by the remainder of the squadron on 7 December — primarily to relieve detached Flights of Nos 45 and 208 Squadrons so that these could return to their Egyptian bases. The purpose of this detachment was a crop of recent Jewish-Arab riots and the consequent need for reinforcement of the area.

No 208 Squadron, in the interim, had moved base from Ismailia to Heliopolis in October 1927,

Below:
No 208 Squadron over characteristic Egyptian landscape. *MoD (Air); H857*

being fully established there by 27 October. Here the unit became much involved in close liaison with local army formations, and carried out a series of successful experiments with the use of W/T and R/T towards more efficient army co-operation roles. When fighting broke out in Palestine between the Jewish and Arab populations in August 1929, a composite Flight of four Bristol F2Bs of No 208 Squadron, commanded by Flt Lt J. J. Lloyd-Williams MC, was sent to Ramleh on 17 September. From Ramleh these F2Bs flew daily recce sorties over the disturbed areas and took prompt action when any people were spotted deliberately burning or plundering villages. By the time this detachment was relieved by No 6 Squadron its four F2Bs had made 162 flights involving 208 flying hours. Back at base at Heliopolis again, the whole of No 208 Squadron resumed its routine duties of army liaison — flying 856 hours, or slightly more than 20% of its annual total during the training season of 1929-30 — but on 14 April 1930 a new commanding officer, Sqn Ldr Maurice Moore OBE, took up his appointment and within the following month the squadron began exchanging its obsolescent Bristol F2Bs for Armstrong Whitworth Atlas aircraft.

Even as No 208 Squadron commenced relinquishing its doughty F2Bs, No 6 Squadron's crews were back in action. In February 1930 the borderlands of Transjordan erupted when Ibn Rachid of Hail made it known that if internal factions in Palestine would revolt he would lead a force of 14,000 Arabs across the border to help fight Palestinian Jews. No 6 Squadron sent detached Flights to the area and helped to nullify this threat. Then, in the autumn of 1930, Sheikh Mahmoud made his final bid to establish his sovereignty of the Kurdish state by crossing from Persia into Iraq and gathering to him a large force of dissidents. At that moment in time Iraq was on the verge of becoming an independent state and member of the League of Nations, and therefore it was decided to use Iraqi troops only, albeit with air support by the RAF, to quell the uprising. Throughout the winter of 1930-31 actions and counteractions in the uprising proved indecisive on either side, and from mid-March 1931 aerial bombing attacks on Mahmoud's camps and village-refuges were intensified, resulting in successful dispersal of Mahmoud's forces, and ultimately the personal surrender of the Sheikh on 13 May 1931. Flown by the RAF to Ur, Mahmoud was received with a certain amount of formal ceremony, and then banished permanently from the country — his 16-year campaign against the British and Iraqi governments at an end.

On 10 June 1931 two Fairey Gordon aircraft, K1729 and K1730, arrived on No 6 Squadron as the first examples of the unit's re-equipment from Bristol F2Bs, and within the following four weeks the unit's F2Bs had been honourably retired from service as No 6 Squadron's crews worked up their new Gordons for the equally new official role as a bomber unit. Thereafter only a handful of individual F2Bs lingered on in the Middle East theatre, usually as trainers or hack communication machines — proud veterans of a family which had played a leading part in maintaining the uneasy peace in the zone for almost 14 years.

Below:
The old order changeth . . . F2B FR4744 with Fairey Gordon K1730 at Ismailia, Egypt in April 1932. This Gordon was one of the first two such aircraft delivered to No 6 Squadron to begin replacement of the unit's well-worn Bristol F2Bs. At left is the airship tower built at Ismailia in anticipation of regular airship service from England to India in the 1920s.

Colourful Biffs

This page:
Two views of F2B B1288 in 1918, in fishy livery.

Below:
Candy-striped F2Bs of No 141 Squadron at Biggin Hill, in late 1918.

Below centre:
Maj Brian E. Baker, OC No 141 Squadron, at Biggin Hill in 1918. His F2B, E2604, bears a red rooster on its fin, indicating his unit's claim as 'Cock-of-the-Walk' Squadron.

Bottom:
C4879, *The Crocodile*, at No 7 Training Squadron, Netheravon. It also served briefly with No 40 Squadron. *G. Stuart Leslie*

Top:
A striped-nosed F2B trainer, snapped at Turnberry by Maj J. T. B. McCudden VC.
Via C. C. H. Cole

Above:
F4440, a presentation aircraft, *Darbangha No 1*, at Bickendorf, Cologne in 1919, while serving with No 8 Squadron.

Below:
H1441 at Fermoy in 1920, possibly with No 106 Squadron. *G. Stuart Leslie*

Above right:
F4380, allocated to No 105 Squadron but possibly with No 106 Squadron here, in 1920.

Right:
Depot Bullshine. Tasteful artwork on an F2B at RAF Aboukir, Egypt in the 1920s.

Below:
F4392 'B' at Aboukir, Egypt. *M. Proctor*

Civil Sons

The change-over from war to peace at the close of 1918 opened a new era in aviation as a host of private and official concerns hastened to establish flying as a commercial and/or sporting undertaking. Most aviation companies continued fulfilling wartime contracts for production of Service aircraft for a very short time, but as the bulk of such contracts came to be somewhat abruptly cancelled by government authorities, such firms made prompt attempts to modify their existing stockpiles of aeroplanes for purely peaceful purposes. On 11 January 1919 the ex-RAF Chief of Air Staff, Maj-Gen Sir Frederick Sykes, was appointed as Controller-General of a new Civil Aviation Department of the Air Ministry, which came into being per se on 12 February 1919. At that time aerial carriage of mail, freight and passengers et al was being undertaken chiefly by RAF crews and units, but Sykes wasted little time in acquiring aircraft for civil roles, and in January 1919 requested, among others, three production Bristol F2Bs (H1687, H1688 and H1689) to be stripped of all war impedimenta and be delivered as communications two-seaters with dual controls and — with extra tankage — an endurance of at least five hours. At the same time another F2B, H1460, was modified to have a large hinged cover over its rear cockpit and, titled Coupé, was purchased by the Air Board for VIP transportation on 19 May 1919.

While a number of standard production F2Bs were kept aside for possible RAF use on squadrons, many F2Bs were acquired by the Aircraft Disposal Co (ADC) in 1919-20 and were completely overhauled for hoped-for sales to British and foreign buyers. At least four such F2Bs — H1376, H1639, H1638 and H951 — were civil-registered as G-EASH, G-EASU, G-EASV

Below:
Type 29 Tourer G-EAXA, built in May 1921 with dual controls, was eventually used as a demonstrator and converted to Type 81 Puma standard before finally crashing on 10 May 1924. *Bristol Aeroplane Co*

Above:
Type 47 Tourer G-EART, a three-seater nicknamed *The Honeymoon Express*, in the livery on the Instone Co airline, in 1920.
Bristol Aeroplane Co

Below:
A Type 28 Tourer three-seater, with 230hp Siddeley-Puma engine and hinged rear cockpit cover. *Bristol Aeroplane Co*

Bottom:
Seen in 1920 is Type 29 Tourer G-EAIZ, a two-seater with 230hp Siddeley-Puma engine.
Bristol Aeroplane Co

Above:
Type 36 Seely Puma G-EAUE, built in 1920, was eventually refitted with a Jupiter engine at the RAE, Farnborough and re-serialled J7004.
Bristol Aeroplane Co

and G-EAWA respectively in 1920 as sales demonstration machines for the ADC, and all four were bought initially by Handley Page Ltd at a nominal £800 apiece. Fitted with either Falcon III or 300hp Hispano Suiza engines, by the end of 1923 a total of 22 such F2Bs had entered the British Civil Aircraft Register, while others had been sold and/or ferried to other countries in Europe et al. In 1931, when all Marks of the Bristol F2B were officially declared obsolete for Service use, a number of ex-RAF machines, thoroughly reconditioned, were offered for public sale, with the result that 21 more F2Bs came on to the British Civil Register. One of these was D8096. Built originally at Brislington in May 1918, it was first delivered to the RAF on 20 June 1918. Over the next 15 years D8096 underwent several reconditionings, converting its airframe from Mk I to Mk II and then Mk III (dual) standard, serving with No 208 Squadron RAF and other units in between these return visits to its alma mater at Bristol. Offered for public purchase by 1934, D8096 was initially bought by Capt C. P. B. Ogilvie for civil conversion, and the civil registration G-AEPH was allocated to, but never actually applied on, the F2B. In the event the proposed civilianisation work was not carried out and D8096 spent many years languishing in various shelters and garages until discoverd in 1949 in an old hangar at Elstree aerodrome. It was promptly acquired by the Shuttleworth Trust and, on 11 October 1950, returned again to Filton for a 100% overhaul and restoration to full flying standard. On 14 February 1951 Bristol's chief test pilot, A. J. 'Bill' Pegg, made the refurbished F2B's first air test — the first of numerous flights made since when D8096, in its former RAF livery and restored as nearly as possible to Mk II standard, has continued to thrill literally millions of spectators as the sole surviving, flying example of the Bristol F2B Fighter under the aegis of the Shuttleworth Collection based at Old Warden airfield in Bedfordshire.

The more direct applications of the basic F2B design by Bristol designers for civil aviation fell broadly into four categories, if one includes the ex-H1460 Coupé, retrospectively called Bristol Type 27. The main category of such civil conversions came under the generic title of Tourer, and the initial example of this 'class' was simply an F2B airframe fitted with a 230hp Siddeley Puma engine (taken from a Bristol Badger X crashed by Barnwell on 22 May 1919) and civil-registered as G-EAIZ on 7 August 1919, receiving its Certificate of Airworthiness on 16 September that same year. Used principally as a Bristol Co hack aircraft, G-EAIZ was a dual-controlled, two-seat, open cockpit, civilianised standard F2B with a lower-power engine for reasons of economy. A second similar Tourer, G-EANR, was completed and registered on 23 September in good time for its exhibition at the Paris Salon in December 1919. Thereafter Tourers appeared as two-seat or three-seat, open or enclosed cockpit, variants, many of which went abroad to Spain, Australia, Canada, Greece and Bulgaria eventually. Two of these open cockpit, three-seat machines were modified to have interchangeable wheeled or twin-float undercarriage assemblies for anticipated export purchase, though ultimately these remained unsold.

Several individual Tourers proved to be interesting examples of the designers' attempts to stretch a standard F2B's basic construction to practicable limits. One such was the retrospectively numbered Type 36 Bristol Seely Puma, built specifically for an Air Ministry development competition for light commercial aircraft held at

Below:
Type 81 Puma dual control trainer G-EBFS of the Filton Reserve Flying School. *C. H. Barnes*

Martlesham Heath on 3 August 1920. While in other respects the Seely Puma retained F2B-/Tourer-type wings, undercarriage and Puma engine, its fuselage was given a much deeper, near elephantine outline and an enlarged fin. Its cockpit for the passengers had a hinged cover, and a steel skid was added to the undercarriage to obviate any tendency to nose-over when its Ferodo brakes were applied. The Seely failed to impress the competition judges and it became a test-bed at Filton in the following years for various engine developments before being handed over to the Royal Aircraft Establishment at Farnborough in 1928, fitted with an experimental Jupiter engine, re-titled as Type 85, and given the serial J7004.

One Type 29 Tourer, G-EAXA, a two-seater built in May 1921 with dual controls for evaluation as a possible training machine, was eventually used by the company as a demonstrator before crashing on 10 May 1924. It nevertheless set a pattern for a further 15 Tourers, converted to Types 81 and 88. Of these, four were dual control trainers — G-EBFR, G-EBFS, G-EBFT and G-EBFU — for the Filton Reserve Flying School, with the latter pair fitted with oleo undercarriages. In May 1925 the Greek government bought six of these Tourers (Bristol seq Nos 6712-6717 inclusive). All were fitted with oleo undercarriages, strengthened tail-skids, balanced ailerons and rudders, a camera mounting, but no guns or gun gear; the Greek authorities supplied the Bristol Co with one Puma engine which was fitted into each aircraft in turn during testing prior to delivery. In 1931 all six were converted back to near-F2B normal standard, including provision of a Scarff Ring on the rear cockpits, by the Greek Navy, and bore the Greek national insignia of blue/white/blue roundels and rudder stripes.

The Tourers attracted sales from several other countries, including Bulgaria, Spain, Australia. Bulgaria ordered a total of five machines, fitted with 180hp Wolseley Viper powerplants in two versions, Types 88 and 88A, the latter version having enlarged rudders and night-flying equipment. The first two were delivered in April 1924 — Bristol seq Nos 6383 and 6384 which became registered as B-BECA and B-BEHA respectively — while the remaining three were finally purchased in April 1926, these being seq Nos 6937 (B-BEBA), 6938 (B-BETO) and 6939 (B-BEKA). Five other Tourers, all three-seaters, were bought by Spain in 1921. The first to be air-ferried out were G-EAWQ and G-EAWR, both in April 1921, these being re-marked respectively as M-AAEA and M-AEAA. In September that same year the remaining three were delivered, to become M-AFFA, M-AAAF and M-AFFF. In the same year too Australia purchased a total of eight three-seat Tourers, the first to be delivered being seq No 6117 in June which became marked G-AUCA. Six more were acquired in September — seq Nos 6108 (G-AUDF), 6111 (G-AUDG), 6115 (G-AUDH), 6116 (G-AUDI), 6118 (G-AUDJ; ex-G-EAXK) and 6119 (G-AUDK). The eighth machine was 6113 (G-AUDX). All eventually suffered serious crashes, including G-AUDH in July 1924 which was rebuilt, re-marked as G-AUDZ, and as such survived until February 1931; parts of G-AUCA, which crashed in March 1923, were incorporated in the 'spare' aircraft G-AUDX. One other Tourer to see service in Australia was a conversion of F2B H1248 in 1922-23 which became G-AUEB, and served until April 1928.

Back in England the Bristol Co design team, still seeking to further the useful life of the founding F2B design, fitted a Bristol Jupiter IV engine of 425hp into F2B G-EBCN — an export Type 17A Fighter with oleo undercarriage — and dubbed this latest version Type 76 Jupiter Fighter, civil-regis-

Above:
Type 47 Tourer G-EAWR was delivered to Madrid on 24 April 1921 and re-registered M-AEAA. *C. H. Barnes*

Below:
The three-seater Tourer G-AUDK at Sydney, Australia in 1928, with Charles Kingsford-Smith (standing in the cockpit) watching his passenger, Mrs J. W. Marshall, being assisted to disembark. *C. H. Barnes*

tered afresh as G-EBGF. Two more Type 76 Jupiter Fighters were then built — G-EBHG and G-EBHH — of which G-EBHG was purchased by the Swedish government after its modification to take a ski undercarriage and other cold weather refinements, becoming thereafter referred to commonly as the Swedish Fighter. Serving first with the Swedish Air Force, the aircraft was successively numbered as 4300, 1300 and, in 1932, as 3667, after which it was sold to a private owner and civil-registered as SE-AEE in February 1935, and was wrecked in a crash on 19 September 1937 — the longest surviving Jupiter Fighter.

In 1924 a further variant was produced when Type 81A G-EBIH was given a derated Jupiter III engine to become the 'prototype' Type 89 two-seater advanced trainer, and eight further examples soon followed. These Type 89s had Frise ailerons and enlarged, horn-balanced rudders and fins (similar to the Service F2B Mk IV version), and were employed at the Filton Reserve School and, later, the Renfrew Reserve Flying School. In October 1926 type 89A, G-EBOC, was given a new design of fuselage, using a plywood-covered monocoque construction in place of its former tie-rod bracing arrangement. Completed in black Cerric fuselage colouring with silver-doped wings and tails, G-EBOC and nine other Type 89As were flown at the Filton School — earning themselves the soubriquet 'Black Marias' from their livery — while three more went to the Renfrew School, where a fourth machine, G-EBWN, was built locally from spare components and salvaged items. These 'Black Marias' proved to be the ultimate design derivatives of their parent Bristol F2B, and as such faded from active flying by mid-1935 when the last surviving Type 89As — G-AAGF, G-AALO and G-ABPM — were all officially written off in August.

Above left:
Type 76 Jupiter Fighter G-EBHG with ski undercarriage, in Sweden. *C. H. Barnes*

Left:
Type 81A G-EBIH, which was converted to the 'prototype' Type 89 two-seater advanced Jupiter trainer. *C. H. Barnes*

Above:
Type 89A G-EBOC in its 'Black Maria' livery. *C. H. Barnes*

Below:
This Type 48 Tourer, a three-seater with Puma engine, was one of two float versions originally intended for export to Siberia. It was first air-tested by Cyril Uwins at Avonmouth on 15 October 1920, carrying two passengers and 40lb of ballast. *Bristol Aeroplane Co*

Top:
G-ACFP (ex-F4434) was built originally in October 1918 and eventually modified to Mk IV standard in June 1931; it was the last F2B to be reconditioned at Filton and is seen here when with the Empire Air Services, Hanworth. Its civil registration lapsed on 1 January 1938.
C. H. Barnes

Above:
G-ACCG, ex-J6790, which was ultimately scrapped in July 1939. *C. H. Barnes*

Mods and Modes

Left:
An F2B's Falcon engine undergoing maintenance in 1918.

Above:
A close view of an F2B's gun synchronisation gearing.
E. J. Watkin

Above:
C906, a Sunbeam Arab-engined F2B with SE5-type twin radiators, viewed at Filton in April 1918. *C. H. Barnes*

Below:
H6058 as built by the Austin Motor Co with a Siddeley Puma engine. *C. H. Barnes*

Top:
B1200 was fitted with a 180hp Wolseley Viper and tested at Martlesham Heath from December 1917 to February 1918. *C. H. Barnes*

Above:
B1201, which was fitted experimentally at the RAE with an RAF4D air-cooled engine.
RAE, Farnborough

Left:
An F2B with a parachute stowage container under the fuselage, and 112lb bomb, at the Isle of Grain on 21 September 1918. *G. Stuart Leslie*

Right:
This F2B had been fitted with a steel Leitner-Watts propeller. *G. Stuart Leslie*

Below:
F2B C4654 was used for meteorological research at the RAE, Farnborough. Note the high altitude propeller and the air sampling collector tubing attached to the upper wing.

Top:
F4728 at Farnborough on 25 January 1923, fitted experimentally with three-bay wings of 9.78 aspect ratio. *RAE, Farnborough*

Above:
Falcon-powered F2B F4360, also pictured at Farnborough on 25 January 1923, was fitted experimentally with single-bay wings of 4.69 aspect ratio. This machine saw service with No 2 Squadron RAF in its normal form.
RAE, Farnborough

Left:
Experimenting with a free-flight glider target in the early 1920s.

Top:
Replacing the hitherto traditional three-men style of hand-starting engines came the Hucks Starter, introduced into the RAF officially on 27 May 1920. It comprised a Ford T-Model ('Tin Lizzie') chassis and appropriate gearing/coupling, and in this view is being attached to F2B J6611 at the RAE. *MoD (Air); H67*

Above:
Queen meets a King. HM Queen Mary, visiting St Omer RFC Depot on 5 July 1917, inspects a Bristol F2B. The nearest officer is Maj-Gen Sir Hugh Trenchard GOC, RFC.

From the Cockpits

Unlike the majority of the aircraft they were given to fly to war in 1914-18, the Bristol Fighter received nothing but fulsome praise from its aircrews. Few (if indeed any) demurred from the tribute recorded by Maj Oliver Stewart MC:

'The Bristol Fighter should be spoken of in terms of the heroes of classic mythology. It was, in the fullest sense, a hero after their pattern — a fighter by name, inclination and aptitude . . . there were no odds which the Bristol Fighters refused to tackle . . . the pilot could enter a dogfight and turn almost as quickly and on almost as small a radius as the best single-seater. He could fling his machine about, go into vertical dives, pull it out quickly, turn it on its back, spin it, roll it, and generally do every sort of manoeuvre if the need arose.' (*The Clouds Remembered*, by L. Bridgman & O. Stewart; 1936.)

Or, as one Australian pilot described it:

'The Bristol Fighter, or "Bif", was a pretty two-seater biplane entirely devoid of tricks. She would not take a mean advantage of you by putting herself into a spin when least expected. She had a good turn of speed, good manoeuvrability, and could carry a good load. In horsy language, she had a mouth of velvet, perfect manners, and no vices.' (*Aces and Kings*, by L. W. Sutherland; J. Hamilton, 1936.)

Another, who flew F2Bs in action as 'B' Flight commander with No 22 Squadron in 1918, was Capt (later Major) W. F. J. Harvey MBE, DFC & Bar, TD, who described the F2B as:

'. . . a classic aeroplane, in looks, in performance for its period, and of a curiously perfect tactical design at a time when the future requirements of a fighting aircraft were not fully understood, nor the strategy and tactics of fighting in the air fully developed. . . . The back-to-back seating of pilot and rear gunner, classic position of those fighting against odds, made possible instant change from offence to defence, and back again. So close was the seating that an experienced Bristol war-flying pilot could be recognised by the scar across the back of his (leather) flying coat, caused by friction from the Scarff gun mounting. And the point of an elbow into the rear gunner's kidney would spur him into action quicker than any intercom.' (*Pi in the Sky*, by W. F. J. Harvey, 1969.)

'Jim' Harvey's opinion of the F2B was enhanced by his personal observations over many months of first-line operations, and included a number of facets of his F2B's abilities not to be found in any official manual. Among these were a climb by five F2Bs with full war load to 20,350ft — and still climbing — before oxygen lack and freezing cold necessarily halted the climb; while at near ground level an F2B without war load, and 100cwt of ballast in place of the gunner, maintained straight and level flight despite six of its Falcon's 12 cylinders being out of action. On another occasion, when about to be attacked by 15 Fokker D VII fighters while on a solitary patrol, Harvey put his F2B into a steep dive with his throttle wide open. As he plunged near-vertically he saw his Air Speed Indicator (ASI) complete 2½ total revolutions of the dial, then break — reaching a speed calculated later at between 234 and 245mph — before he finally pulled out of the dive sharply, and attacked one of four AEG two-seaters engaged in strafing Allied infantry, shooting down one AEG which presented a full deflection shot, then coming out of his headlong dive abruptly. The pull-out caused Harvey to 'grey out' momentarily from the gravity-pull, while his gunner's seat collapsed under the G-force. Reaching his base airfield safely, Harvey found the F2B's rigging somewhat disarrayed, the steel main member of the tail distorted, while the propeller boss had a neat, surrounding circle of bullet holes where his diving speed had over-run the normal operation of the forward gun's synchronisation gear.

Harvey's admiration of the Bristol F2B was

Above:
The crew of F2B A7107 '6' of the Wireless Experimental Establishment at Biggin Hill in 1918. This F2B originally served with No 48 Squadron in April-August 1917.
RAF Museum; P7137

shared universally among the RFC and RAF aircrews. Lt Vivian Voss, who was to serve throughout most of 1918 with Nos 48 then 88 Squadrons, recalled his first acquaintance with the F2B while under instruction at Netheravon:

'Lt Dobbie, who was killed later in Egypt, flew me twice round the aerodrome in a Bristol. There was no dual control in this. The pilot sat in the front cockpit and the observer in the rear one. He took off in a great climbing turn, with a split-ass turn at the top. When we landed, he said, "All right, take her up, but don't do any climbing turns." So I climbed over into the pilot's seat and opened the throttle. I felt at home at once in a Bristol even on this first solo. The engine, a 250hp Rolls-Royce, was infinitely more powerful than anything I had come across so far. It gave a full-throated roar and shot away across the aerodrome and then up, soaring into the air like a great eagle. She was a massive machine but so beautifully designed that she did not feel heavy on the controls. She responded superbly to the least touch of the stick or rudder bar. After flying round for half an hour, I brought her down and landed quite smoothly. I felt that up to the present I had only been playing at flying. (*Flying Minnows*, by 'Roger Vee'; J. Hamilton, 1935.)

What of the F2B Observer-gunners? In the early years of the aerial war aerial gunners (as opposed to Observers) were in the main non-commissioned personnel drawn from the 'rankers' on each squadron, usually on a volunteer basis, and by 1917 and the introduction of the Bristol F2B this arrangement still prevailed to a large extent, although by then the aircrew category of Observer (for officers only initially) had been inaugurated from August 1915. A qualified Observer was awarded his winged-O breast badge after satisfying a number of prerequisites, particularly after completing at least 50 flying hours on actual war sorties 'over enemy lines' — a qualification which many gunners never lived to achieve. A. G. J. Whitehouse — 'Arch' — transferred as a Private from the Northamptonshire Yeomanry to the RFC to become an aerial gunner in late 1916, and was posted to No 22 Squadron RFC. Although Whitehouse was well qualified in the knowledge and use of all standard Army machine guns of the period, he had never flown in an aeroplane, nor was he to receive any formal training in aerial gunnery tactics — he was airborne and in combat within mere hours of his arrival on the squadron, swinging the Lewis gun attached to his plywood nacelle 'bathtub' cockpit up front of an FE23B two-seater 'pusher'. In July-August 1917 the unit began receiving F2Bs in place of its well-worn FEs and Whitehouse and his fellow gunners had to re-adjust their tactical experience to rear-seat defence and offence — and the fact that the superior performance of the F2B meant longer and higher patrols thereafter. By the winter of 1917-18 No 22 Squadron's F2B crews had established a fine reputation in their new warhorses, but the physical problems remained acute.

'Flying was agony. Not from the angle of danger, or Jerry, or archie. It was the cold. All our work was now carried out at 18,000ft, and once we did a show at 23,000. It was bitter cold, and we all went around with blue-green splotches on our cheeks as the result of frost-bite. We smothered ourselves with whale-oil and stunk to high Heaven. They brought out the first electrically-heated Sidcot flying suits, but the pilots, who sat up close to the engine, were the first to get them. I wore two sweaters under my tunic, a pair of long woollen stockings that came up over my thighs, a smaller pair of boot socks, and fleece-lined flying boots that reached to my hips. I wore a woollen helmet under my issue leather one and used to wrap a six-foot scarf around my neck. Silk gloves went on under regular woollen ones, and over that we drew our regular leather flying gloves, which had a fold-over mitten to protect the fingers when we were not using the guns. Still, I was never so cold in all my life.' (*Hell in the Heavens*, by A. G. J. Whitehouse MM; W. & R. Chambers, 1938.)

The problem of operating the rear gunner's Lewis gun in F2Bs was exacerbated at any good altitude. From 8-10,000ft sheer lack of oxygen made quick physical movement of the gun and its Scarff Ring a painful, slow affair, while higher altitudes often rendered F2B rear defences near-helpless. Many other types of two-seat aircraft often employed twin yoked Lewis guns on the rear Scarff mounting, eg RE8s and Armstrong Whitworth FK8s, but these machines were employed primarily on relatively low-level reconnaissance and bombing sorties. To attempt to swing the double weight of yoked Lewis guns — dubbed 'Huntley and Palmer' by the gunners — at higher heights proved near impossible. Nevertheless, an F2B's arc of fire was greatly wider than any other type of aircraft. The sloping rear fuselage gave only small blind spots behind or below the tail, while the setting of the upper wing so close to the fuselage enabled gunners to fire forward above the pilot's head — *if* they remembered that the revolving propeller was in that direction! Apart from the obvious dangers from enemy bullets, gunners were subjected to other hazards once an F2B became embroiled in close dogfighting. By mid-1917 F2B pilots had evolved the general tactic of flying the aircraft like a single-seat fighter, with the added advantage of a rear gun. This meant that pilots manoeuvred violently and rapidly, leaving the unfortunate gunner to carry on firing when required from physical positions seldom encountered in other types of two-seat aircraft.

In a majority of F2Bs the rear gunner was seldom, if ever, strapped into his seat or cockpit, relying entirely on jamming his feet, legs, and body against the sides of his cockpit, and keeping a firm grip on his Lewis gun. Inevitably, perhaps, a number of gunners were thrown out of their fragile cockpits in moments of high tension during any wildly manoeuvring combat. One such luckless gunner was Capt J. H. Hedley flying with Lt Makepeace in an F2B, A7255, of No 20 Squadron RFC on 6 January 1918. While flying at 15,000ft the F2B became involved in a brief clash with enemy fighters, during the course of which Makepeace suddenly stood the F2B on its nose in a rapid dive. As he pulled the F2B out again he felt a distinct thump in the fuselage behind him, and on glancing back over his shoulder was astonished to see his gunner, Hedley, clinging by fingers and boots to the top of the rear fuselage beyond his usual cockpit. Hedley had a waist strap buckled on initially but had undone this as combat was joined and, when Makepeace made his sudden dive, had been catapulted clean out of the cockpit into thin air. By the sheerest coincidental chance Hedley's falling body had arrived at exactly the same point in space as the F2B when this pulled out of its dive. Hedley remained clinging for dear life in his precarious position until Makepeace regained their base airfield — only to be mildly rebuked by his unit commander for 'endangering the aircraft structure' by having punched finger and toe holes in the fuselage fabric! Hedley's escape from a particularly horrific death recalls one verse of a contemporary ditty titled 'The P.B.O's Lament' — PBO standing for Poor Bloody Observer. Sung to the music of 'A Bachelor Gay' from the musical comedy 'Maid of the Mountains', the verse ran:

'We all of us know the case
When the pilot comes home alone
No doubt it was only a slight mistake
But his attitude's clearly shown

He shoved his joystick suddenly down
As far as it would go;
"Hello, you seem to have gone", he said
"I fear you must be somewhat dead",
"But you're only a PBO, yes, you're only a PBO".

Hedley's luck held out for a further 11 weeks, until 27 March 1918 when, flying as gunner to Capt K. R. Kirkham in F2B B1156, he and his pilot were shot down by the German 'Ace of aces', Rittmeister Manfred von Richthofen near Foucaucourt and both men became prisoners of war.

In the immediate postwar years the drastically reduced RAF, championed by Hugh Trenchard, had to contend with parsimonious and reluctant governmental financial and moral support, and the existing squadrons had to be content with continuing use of wartime-produced aircraft with which to fulfil fully operational roles in many British Empire countries and other mandated territories. Initially the onus of responsibility for such roles fell heavily upon two types of aircraft, the de Havilland 9A, or 'Ninak', and the Bristol F2B, both of these designs remaining in first-line squadron use for a decade or more after the 1918 Armistice. The F2B's specific roles in the postwar RAF was designated as Army Co-operation; a description sufficiently vague in definition to permit the inclusion of myriad tasks never envisaged for the aircraft by Frank Barnwell. Pilots' opinions of the F2B on first-line units flying operations overseas are included in chapters 'India, 1918-32' and 'Middle East, 1918-32', but in the UK Bristol F2Bs formed several of the early army co-operation squadrons until the late 1920s brought replacements of (in the main) Armstrong Whitworth Atlas aircraft. Allen Wheeler (later, Air Commodore CBE, MA) was first commissioned in the RAF in January 1924, was trained to fly Avro 504s and Bristol F2Bs at Digby, then joined No 2 (AC) Squadron to fly more F2Bs. His first impressions of flying an F2B are recorded in his delightful part-autobiography *Flying between the Wars* (G. T. Foulis, 1972).

Below:
A post-1918 F2B crew demonstrating the age-old traditional two-man 'back-to-back' fighting stance epitomised in the Bristol Fighter design. *MoD (Air); H66*

'The first thing impressed on us was respect for the engine — no "blipping" for instance. One opened up the engine gently and it always seemed to give its full power. The water coolant temperature had to be watched, and controlled with the radiator shutters. . . . The pre-take-off check was fairly simple. After running up and checking oil pressure, water temperature, both magnetos, and take-off revs, one merely set the "cheese-cutter" tail adjustment, wiggled all the controls to their full movement to check that they came to "meet the stick" in every case lest some mechanic had replaced one since the last flight and crossed the wires, and then one taxied out. Taxying in a light wind was fairly easy. There were no brakes, but the tail skid gave enough braking effect to need significant engine power before the aircraft moved, thus ensuring a fair slipstream over the rudder. Taxying down-wind was more tricky but use of the ailerons augmented the rudder control very effectively if they were operated as for a normal turn in the air. In this way the following wind acted on the "down" ailerons and helped the rudder. Taxying into wind required aileron operation the other way.

'Take-off was absolutely straightforward, with very little tendency to swing, and the Bristol Fighter flew itself off in a quietly graceful way which was a joy to watch and hear. It was very stable with rather heavy controls all round. We were told that the elevators were made specially heavy since the specification called for a maximum diving speed at 400mph, and light elevators at that speed could have been embarrassing. I doubt if the Bristol could have reached such a figure even in a vertical dive, but it certainly picked up speed very quickly in a shallow dive at full power — as for a loop, which one entered at speeds between 120 and 140mph. Its spin characteristics were normal, but a lot of height was lost during recovery owing to the steep angle of spinning and the aircraft's relatively heavy weight. One of the most impressive aerobatic manoeuvres practised in the Bristol was the flick roll, induced by adjusting the speed to approximately 85mph in level flight and pulling the stick hard back with full rudder; it then did an impressive one turn of a spin horizontally, following which the pilot quickly normalised the controls to prevent it starting another. A "falling leaf" was also possible, and quite neat, but one had to use a little engine power during the change-over to keep the manoeuvre symmetrical. As in the Avro (504) a slow roll was virtually impossible owing to the very heavy ailerons; furthermore, we only had lap straps in the Bristol Fighter.

'Approach and landing was very straight-forward. It stalled at 42mph and the approach correction was greatly assisted by the wonderful control one had even in the steepest side-slip. We looked upon the Bristol landing run as rather long — all of 100 yards on a calm day — but the grass aerodromes we operated from as pupils usually gave a landing or take-off run of at least 900 yards, often much more. In operational squadrons we were expected to operate from 400-yard strips with reasonably clear approaches.

'Within three weeks from first solo most of us were doing all normal aerobatics and had started practising cloud flying. One had, of course, no sophisticated instruments in those days for blind flying. One kept the angle of climb or descent reasonably constant by watching the ASI and kept the aeroplane level laterally by partly trusting to its own natural stability provided by a generous dihedral angle of the wings and partly — but very doubtfully — by reference to the "bubble" which worked on the ordinary builders' level principle, but the bubble tube was curved to make it less sensitive to minor deviations. Since this "bubble" instrument was very sensitive to accelerations due to flat turns one was never very sure in a cloud whether it was indicating a side-slip or a flat turn. For such reasons, in our early cloud flying practices, we wisely selected very thin layers of cloud, flew as fast as the Bristol would go just below the cloud and then pulled up to a good climbing angle hoping to emerge above the cloud before losing control. As confidence increased we tried flying level in cloud and surprisingly became fairly good at it. But even experienced pilots hesitated to go into cloud unless the cloud base was high enough above ground level to allow for recovery from a spin after emerging. Aeroplanes in those days had the advantage that they were stressed to be able to dive vertically, and pulling out of a very steep dive, even in a Bristol Fighter, could be achieved in under 1,000ft if one pulled hard enough. . . . From then on our training consisted largely of cross-country flights which, on occasions, included landing at another aerodrome, usually Spittlegate, near Grantham, where there was another FTS. We also improved our aerobatics which included loops, half-rolls, flick rolls, spins, and the "falling leaf". Inverted flying was not allowed on the Bristol Fighter.'

Some 40 years after Allen Wheeler's introduction to the F2B, another pilot, Godfrey Auty, the Bristol Co's Chief Test Pilot, made his first flight in F2B D8096 at Cranfield, and his personal impressions illustrate vividly the affection for the design felt by all generations of F2B crews:

'From the moment of placing one's left foot on the root of the lower port wing to hoist oneself into the cockpit there is a feeling of unity between man and the machine. The homely comfort of a basket seat with leather-covered cushion is soon forgotten, however, on seeing the holes in the fabric through which the bracing wires pass and allow cold air to blow on the pilot's legs and feet. The Rolls-Royce Falcon engine is started easily by a chain of three men pulling the propeller over a compression stroke, while the pilot winds the starting magneto. The engine ticks over at 700rpm; this generates — at first — quite an alarming clatter but as speed is increased the noise becomes less noticeable. After entering the cockpit there are only 15 checks to make before take-off. Take-off is normally made into the wind, but small cross-winds present no problem. Once the throttle has been eased fully open, the tail of the aircraft is raised by forward pressure on the stick, then in a matter of seconds a gentle rearward movement of the stick has the aircraft flying at 45mph with the speed quickly increasing to climbing speed 65mph. Take-off distance varies but 200 yards is ample.

'Climbing at full throttle and 65mph gives a rate of climb of 1,000ft a minute. Re-adjustment of the tailplane incidence control is all that is necessary to make the aircraft fly "hands-off". In cruising flight the aircraft can be flown for long periods during which the pilot has only to keep an eye on water temperature and oil pressure. With 1,800-1,900rpm a speed of 85mph is achieved. The Bristol Fighter is fully aerobatic but is most suited to the looping plane; the ailerons are heavy and create a lot of drag when fully applied for rolling the aircraft. A close watch must be kept on the revs when diving as engine speed increases with airspeed. Any reasonably smooth field can be used for landing. The approch is made, with power on or off, at 55-60mph. Speed is then reduced to 45mph and the aircraft held in the three-point attitude to settle on the ground for a smooth landing. Too much speed when the wheels touch the ground or too big a drop on to the ground and the rubber bungees of the undercarriage catapult the aircraft into the air like a kangaroo.'

Below:
Last of an illustrious line, still flying: D8096 of the Shuttleworth Collection, airborne over its base airfield at Old Warden, Bedfordshire.

Appendices

1. Bristol F2A/F2B Serial Batches (UK)

Serials	*Makers*	*Totals*	*Remarks*
F2A			
A3303 & A3304	Bristol Co	2	Prototypes
A3305-A3354	Bristol Co	50	
F2B			
A7101-A7300	Bristol Co	200	
B1101-B1350	Bristol Co	250	
C751-C1050	Bristol Co	300	
C4601-C4900	Bristol Co	300	
C9836-C9985	Gloucestershire Aircraft Co	150	
D2126-D2251	National A/C Factory No 3, Aintree	126	Of original order for 500 a/c
D2626-D2775	Marshall & Sons	150	
D7801-D8100	Bristol Co	300	
E1901-E2150	Armstrong Whitworth	250	
E2151-E2650	Bristol Co	500	
E2651-E2900	Angus Sanderson	250	Mainly delivered to store
E5179-E5428	Standard Motor Co	130	E5253-5308 transferred to Bristol Co
E9507-E9656	Gloucestershire Aircraft Co	150	
F4271-F4970	Bristol Co	700	
F5074-F5173	Harris & Sheldon	100	Mainly delivered direct to store
H926-H1060	Gloucestershire Aircraft Co	135	Of original order for 250 a/c
H1240-H1739	Bristol Co	500	H1708-1739 not completed
H6055 & H6058	Austin Motor Co	2	Of original order for 600 a/c
J6586-J6800	Bristol Co	215	First postwar order
J7570		1	Built locally, but serial duplicated
J7616-J7699	Bristol Co	84	Originally to Mk II standard
J8242-J8291	Bristol Co	50	Originally to Mk III(AC) standard
J8429-J8458	Bristol Co	30	Last postwar order

NB: Cancelled contracts et al excluded for ease of reference.

Miscellaneous statistics
By 31 October 1918, of a gross total of 1,754 machines actually delivered to RAF units, a total of 1,583 F2Bs (all types) remained on strength, distributed as follows:

In United Kingdom
In transit or at ARDS: 83
In store: 517
At AAPs or contractors: 147
Squadrons mobilising: 3
Areas: 206
Schools: 82
6th Brigade (HD): 58
Sundry Units: 24
CTD: 19

Overseas
Expeditionary Force, France: 328
14th Wing, Italy: 48
Egypt and Palestine: 42
Awaiting shipment and/or assembly: 26

2. Known Rebuilt F2Bs

Rebuilding and thereby reserialling aircraft by the RFC and RAF during the period 1914-18 became virtually a minor industry, creating no small confusion to subsequent archivists and historians. The following serials, though not within normal production serial batches, are known to have been allotted to rebuilt F2Bs, but should not be regarded as any comprehensive listing. Additions and/or corrections will be welcomed by this author.

Serial	*Remarks*
B817	– No 20 Squadron, 1918
B883	– No 20 Squadron, 1918
B7763	– 200hp Hispano-Suiza engine
B7781	– 230hp BHP engine
B7947	– '5' of No 88 Squadron
B8914	– 200hp Arab engine; to No 11 Squadron 28/1/18; to No 12 Squadron 2/2/18
B8915	– Arab engine; Martlesham Heath, February-June 1918
8919	– No 35(T) Squadron, Port Meadow, March 1918
B8923	
B8925	– '18' at Rendcombe, 1918
B8928	– Eastchurch
B8937	– Crashed and burned out, 1919
B8941	– No 11 Squadron, September 1918
B8943	
B8947	– Eastchurch
B8948	– No 45 TDS, Rendcombe
C4548	– Rebuilt by No 18 Wing ARS; No 1 School of Aerial Gunnery (Observers), Hythe
E9971	
F5809	– To No 48 Squadron, 29/6/18
F5810	
F5811	– '3' of No 48 Squadron
F5812	– No 62 Squadron; 'L' Flight
F5813	
F5814	– No 11 Squadron, September 1918
F5815	– In France 30/6/18
F5817	– No 48 Squadron
F5819	– 'L' Flight, August 1918
F5820	– No 22 Squadron; SOC 11/9/18
F5821	
F5822	– 'L' Flight
F5823	– No 22 Squadron
F5824	– No 22 Squadron
F5995	– No 48 Squadron
F5996	– 'P', No 24 Squadron, 1919
F5997	– No 6 Squadron; No 88 Squadron
F5998	– B1314 rebuilt 24/7/18

Serial	*Remarks*
F5999	– C4699 rebuilt 24/7/18; No 88 Squadron, 1918
F6040	– C882 rebuilt 24/7/18
F6041	– C920 rebuilt 25/7/18
F6042	– C781 (ex-No 5 Squadron) rebuilt 25/7/18
F6043	– C929 (ex-No 22 Squadron) rebuilt 30/7/18
F6093	
F6094	– No 48 Squadrons
F6101	
F6116	– No 20 Squadrons, missing in action (MIA) 1/11/18
F6121	– 'S', No 20 Squadron
F6131	– No 11 Squadron, September 1918
F6142	
F6158	
F6195	– C4847 (ex-No 11 Squadron) rebuilt 17/7/18; No 20 Squadron and MIA 10/11/18
F6206	– B1271 (ex-No 48 Squadron) rebuilt 18/7/18; No 11 Squadron
F6208	– D7911 rebuilt 22/7/18
F6217	– C792 rebuilt 25/7/18
F6235	
F9516	– E2460 rebuilt August 1918
F9549	
F9606	– No 59 Squadron, 1919
F9616	– No 5 Squadron; No 20 Squadron
F9638	– School of Army Co-operation, Winchester
H6893	– C9896 rebuilt
H7060	– 'F6400' renumbered*
H7061	– 'F6401' renumbered; No 12 Squadron
H7062	– 'F6402' renumbered; No 22 Squadron
H7063	– 'F6403' renumbered
H7064	– 'F6404' renumbered
H7065	– 'F6406' renumbered; No 62 Squadron and SOC 21/3/19
H7069	– B1209 (ex-Nos 20 and 22 Squadrons) rebuilt
H7070	– B1234 (ex-Nos 10, 48, 62 and 88 Squadrons) rebuilt
H7171	– ex-A7256 of No 20 Squadron
H7172	– B1307 (ex-Nos 11 and 20 Squadrons) rebuilt
H7173	– C842 (ex-No 22 Squadrons) rebuilt
H7174	– C4746 (ex-No 62 Squadron) rebuilt
H7175	– C4817 rebuilt
H7196	– C868 rebuilt
H7197	– C983 (ex-No 88 Squadron) rebuilt
H7198	– D8065 (ex-Nos 139 and 1 AFC Squadrons) rebuilt
H7291	– 'F6405' renumbered
H7292	– 'F6407' renumbered
H7293	– 'F6408' renumbered

Serial	*Remarks*
J5721	– No 4 Squadrons, 1922-23
J5784	– No 4 Squadrons, 1923
J7468†	– No 13 Squadron (duplicated Fairey Flycatcher serial)
J7829†	– No 14 Squadron (duplicated DH9A serial)

*The 'F64--' serials were themselves spurious
†Though recorded per se, probably incorrect documentary entries

NB: These rebuilt F2Bs should not be equated with the various F2Bs refurbished in post-1918 years, usually locally by commands, and then had 'R' added to their serial prefix letters, eg JR6635.

3. Presentation F2Bs 1917-18

The wartime aircraft 'presentation' schemes, whereby private organisations and even individuals provided funds for the 'purchase' of aircraft for the RFC, RNAS and RAF and had machines embellished with appropriate names and/or titles, eventually extended to at least 1,400 aircraft of many types. Of these, at least 101 were recorded as Bristol F2Bs. It should be noted, however, that the presentation 'nameplate' of certain F2Bs was often given to several aircraft in succession, due to attrition of 'original' titled machines as the war progressed. The following list of 101 F2Bs are confirmed as having been marked at some period with presentation titling.

Serial	*Title*	*Remarks*
A7175	*Malaya No 23, The Malacca*	No 11 Squadron, lost 23/8/17
A7176	*Montreal No 4*	No 11 Squadron; No 48 Squadron, crashed 15/9/17
A7177	*Auckland*	No 48 Squadron, lost 11/8/17
A7178	*Australia No 1, The Sidney Kidman*	No 22 Squadron, crashed 18/10/17
A7179	*Johore No 6*	No 22 Squadron, lost 11/8/17
A7180	*Dominica*	No 20 Squadron
A7181	*Newfoundland No 4*	No 22 Squadron; Orfordness
A7182	*Gold Coast No 11*	No 48 Squadron, wrecked 10/9/17
A7190	*Australia No 15, NSW No 14, The Women's Battleplane*	No 111 Squadron; No 1 Squadron AFC
A7200	*Australia No 13, NSW No 12, The Macintyre Kayuga Estate*	No 111 Squadron; No 1 Squadron AFC
A7225	*Ajmeer*	'4' of No 48 Squadron
A7226	*Kotah No 2*	No 11 Squadron; No 22 Squadron
A7236	*Australia No 1, The Sidney Kidman*	No 1 Squadron AFC, lost 27/6/18
A7237	*Australia No 9, NSW No 8*	No 111 Squadron; No 1 Squadron AFC
A7267	*Malaya No 23*	Replaced A7175, 11/10/17
A7299	*Darbhanga No 2*	No 20 Squadron, lost 10/12/17
A7300	*Darbhanga No 4*	'A' of No 22 Squadron; SOC 12/3/18
B1105	*Kotah No 1*	No 22 Squadron, lost 11/9/17
B1107	*Falkland*	No 59 TS, 1917; SOC 6/5/18
B1108	*Udaipur No 2;* also *Jeypores Vizag*	No 48 Squadron, 1918
B1109	*Udaipur No 1*	No 11 Squadron, lost 31/10/17
B1110	*Johore No 2*	No 20 Squadron; No 11 Squadron, crashed 13/1/81
B1111	*Punjab No 44*	Written off 25/3/18
B1114	*Auckland*	Replaced A7177; No 22 Squadron; No 20 Squadron and lost 5/6/18
B1117	*Johore No 6*	Replaced A7179; No 48 Squadron; lost 24/10/17
B1122	*Dominica*	Replaced A7180; No 20 Squadron; crashed 23/6/18
B1143	*Kotah No 1*	Replaced B1105; No 11 Squadron
B1145	*Darbangha No 3*	SOC 11/17
B1146	*Australia No 2, NSW No 1*	No 1 Squadron AFC
B1147	*Australia No 24, South Australia No 2, The Mrs Sidney Kidman*	No 111 Squadron; No 1 Squadron AFC

Serial	*Title*	*Remarks*
B1148	*Australia No 3, NSW No 2, The White Edenglassie*	No 1 Squadron AFC
B1149	*Australia No 11, NSW No 10, Duplicate Tweed No 9*	No 1 Squadron AFC
B1181	*Baroda No 14*	No 48 Squadron, crashed 17/3/18
B1186	*Montreal No 4*	Replaced C4805; No 39 Squadron; No 33 Squadron; to Canada
B1199	*Australia No 10, NSW No 9, The Tweed*	No 1 Squadron AFC
B1223	*Australia No 17, NSW No 16, The Upper Hunter Battleplane*	No 1 Squadron AFC; No 2 Squadron, post-1918
B1229	*Australia No 12, NSW No 11, The Macintyre Kayuga Estate*	No 1 Squadron AFC; to Australia
B1230	*Montreal*	'Z' Flight; No 139 Squadron
B1231	*Winnipeg*	No 88 Squadron; No 48 Squadron
B1232	*Toronto*	No 20 Squadron, lost 16/5/18
B1234	*Edmonton*	No 62 Squadron; No 10 Squadron; No 48 Squadron; No 88 Squadron; rebuilt/reserialled H7070
B1242	*Ajmeer*	Replaced A7225; No 33 TDS
B1262	*Darbhanga No 2*	No 39 Squadron
B1276	*Australia No 18, NSW No 17, The Upper Hunter Battleplane*	No 1 Squadron AFC, lost 13/8/18
B1285	*Australia No 7, NSW No 6, The White Edenglassie*	No 1 Squadron AFC
B1330	*Darbangha No 5*	No 11 Squadron; No 22 Squadron; No 39 Squadron
B1331	*Darbangha No 1*	No 39 Squadron
B1335	*Malaya No 23*	Replaced A7267; No 62 Squadron
C797	*Udiapur No 1*	Replaced C4832; No 11 Squadron
C970	*Malaya No 19, Singapore No 2*	
C989	*Bhopal*	No 20 Squadron; No 22 Squadron
C1034	*Zanzibar No 17*	'L' Flight
C4623	*Australia No 8, NSW No 7, The Mrs P. Kirby & Son*	No 1 Squadron AFC; No 111 Squadron
C4624	*Australia No 13, NSW No 12, The Macintyre Kayuga Estate*	No 67 Squadron RFC
C4626	*Australia No 16, NSW No 15, The Upper Hunter*	No 1 Squadrons AFC
C4627	*City of Adelaide*, presented by Mrs Harry Bickford	No 1 Squadron AFC
C4635	*Darbangha No 3*	Replaced B1145; No 39 Squadron
C4805	*Montreal No 4*	Replaced A7176; No 2 TS; No 35 TS
C4810	*Gold Coast No 11*	Replaced A7182; No 20 Squadron; 'N' of No 22 Squadron and crashed 22/4/18
C4818	*Newfoundland No 4*	A7181; No 20 Squadron, crashed 3/5/18
C4831	*Johore No 6*	Replaced B1117; No 48 Squadron, crashed 10/7/18
C4832	*Udaipur No 1*	No 22 Squadron, lost 30/1/18
C4840	*Australia No 4, NSW No 3, The Mrs P. Kirby & Son*	No 1 Squadron AFC; No 111 Squadron
C4868	*Johore No 2*	Replaced B1110
D2649	*Gold Coast No 14*	No 8 Squadron
D2652	*Malaya No 7, The Armenia*	Replaced Martinsyde G102, 3/10/18
D2660	*Zanzibar No 5*	Replaced FE2b; No 59 Squadron, 1919
D7894	*Kotah No 1*	Replacement; No 22 Squadron, crashed 28/9/18
D7902	*Darbangha No 4*	Replaced A7300; No 48 Squadron and lost 24/7/18
D7913	*Malaya No 23*	Replaced B1335; No 8 Squadron
D7939	*Toronto*	'P', No 20 Squadron, lost 15/9/18
D7942	*Falkland*	Replaced B1107; No 88 Squadron
D7945	*Gold Coast No 11*	Replaced C4810; 62 Squadron, lost 4/9/18

Serial	Title	Remarks
D8061	*Zanzibar No 18*	No 48 Squadron, lost 8/8/18
D8062	*Zanzibar No 19*	No 88 Squadron
D8064	*Zanzibar No 20*	No 88 Squadron, crashed/SOC 20/9/18
D8065	*Australia No 24*	Replaced B1147; No 139 Squadron; No 1 Squadron AFC; rebuilt/re-serialled H7198
E2233	*Alresford Rural District Council*	'B4' of No 12 Squadron, 1919
E2452	*Montreal*	Replacement; No 20 Squadron, crashed 22/8/81
E2453	*Dominica*	Replaced B1122; No 22 Squadron, lost 29/8/18
E2455	*Udaipur No 2*	Replaced B1108; No 48 Squadron, lost 2/9/18
E2457	*Punjab No 44, Lahore No 4*	Replacement; No 62 Squadron
E2525	*Auckland*	Replaced B1114; No 62 Squadron, lost 13/9/18
F4274	*Barnstable (Devon)*	
F4277	*Carlton Colville*	
F4306	*Burgate*	'L' Flight; No 141 Squadron
F4330	*Wingate (County Durham)*	Allocated No 105 Squadron; No 20 Squadron, 1930
F4332	*Forehoe Union (Durham)*	Allocated No 105 Squadron
F4333	*Dominica*	Replaced E2453
F4334	*Montreal*	Replaced E2452; allocated No 105 Squadron; to Canada
F4336	*Zanzibar No 17;* then *Huddersfield, Canada*	No 1 Squadron CAF; became G-CYBC, Canada
F4337	*Zanzibar No 18*	Replaced D8061
F4355	*Darbangha No 4*	
F4440	*Darbangha No 1*	No 18 Squadron, 1919
F4470	*Newfoundland No 4*	No 48 Squadron, 1919
F4537	*Bingley (Yorkshire)*	'V' of No 2 Squadron, post-1918
F4677	*Kotah No 2*	Replaced A7226
F4678	*Winnipeg*	Replaced B1234; to Canada
F4679	*Darbangha No 5*	No 8 Squadron
F4680	*Johore No 6*	Replaced C4831; No 6 Squadron
F4774	*Darbangha No 3*	Replacement: crashed 1919

NB: Acknowledgement for use of original research on presentation aircraft during 1917-18 is gratefully made to Ray Vann and Colin Waugh.

4. Service Use

RFC/RAF Squadrons: Nos 2, 4, 5, 6, 8, 9, 10, 11, 12, 13, 14, 16, 20, 21, 22, 24, 28, 31, 33, 34, 35, 36, 39, 47, 48, 51, 59, 62, 67 (1 AFC), 69 (3 AFC), 70, 75, 76, 88, 100, 105, 106, 111, 114, 138, 139, 140, 141 and 208.

RFC/RAF Flights: L, M, N, O, P, X and Z.

Misc RFC/RAF Units: Nos 1, 2, 4 and 5 Flying Training Schools (FTS); Night Fighting Flight & Wireless Experimental Establishment, Biggin Hill; RAF College, Cranwell; Schools of Army Co-operation Winchester and Old Sarum; No 27 Group, Bircham Newton; RAE & School of Photography, Farnborough; Andover Staff College; No 186 Development Squadron & School of Special Flying, Gosport; Schools of Aerial Gunnery (Observers), Eastchurch, Manston and New Romney; A&AEE, Martlesham Heath; Inland Area Command Flight; Dept of CAS, Northolt; Nos 8, 31 and 35 Training Squadrons; Nos 7 and 8 Training Squadrons AFC; No 1 (Indian) Group, Peshawar; Quetta Station Flight; Palestine Group, Ismailia; Cambridge University Air Squadrons; Oxford UAS; Aden Flight; Central Flying School; No 45 TDS, Rendcombe.

Example F2Bs in squadron/unit 1917-32

No 2 Squadron: B1223; B1325; B1329; C767; F4360; F4366; F4412; F4428; F4484; F4490; F4500; F4537; F4546; F4717; F4854; F4967; H1526; J6592; J6662; J6669; J6694; J6696; J6703; J6794; J7652; J7657; J7667; J7686; J7699; J7899; J8245; J8265; J8267; J8269; J8270.

No 4 Squadron: E2624; F4366; F4412; F4944; H1415; H1420; H1486; H1526; J5721; J5784; J6715; J6719; J6760; J6761; J7654; J7686; J8271; J8275.

No 5 Squadron: C801; C1039; D7830; D8035; D8036; E2421; E2436; E2501; F4320; F4377; F4394; F4403; F4408; F4461; F4463; F4470; F4488; F4498; F4544; F4566; F4592; F4555; F4598; F4607;

F4611; F4614; F4616; F4625; F4627; F4634; F4636; F4637; F4658; F4706; F4746; F4766; F4825; F4861; F4878; F4929; F4947; F4958; F9616; H1461; H1497; H1513; H1515; H1528; H1530; H1544; H1546; H1552; H1565; J6591; J6601; J6613; J6624; J6628; J6631; J6634; J6637; J6641; J6643; J6651; J6653; J6654; J6700; J6715; J6746; J6750; J6759; J6762; J6771; J6772; J6774; J6777.

No 6 Squadron: C766; C923; C1048; C4683; C9879; D7874; DR8056; E2529; E2629; F4362; FR4583; F4590; F4599; FR4600; F4680; F4686; F4691; FR4727; FR4744; F4860; F4880; F4903; FR4925; F4928; F5997; H1464; H1493; H1677; JR6635; J6742; JR6785; J7676; J8281.

No 8 Squadron: A3325; A7143; B1167; C9873; D2649; D7823; D7852; D7879; D7881; D7892; D7898; D7901; D7952; E2649; F4349; F4679; F5110.

No 9 Squadron: B1347; C836; C917; C924; C936; C9879; C9899; C9950; D7947; D7997; E1908; E2150; E2271; E2272; E2569; E9582; E9588; E9595; E9602; E9617; E9642; F5138; F5139.

No 10 Squadron: B1234; C967; C984; E2426.

No 11 Squadron: A7121; A7126; A7128; A7130; A7131; A7134; A7138; A7143; A7145; A7147; A7153; A7154; A7156; A7157; A7159; A7167; A7171; A7174; A7175; A7176; A7191; A7209; A7214; A7226; A7231; A7275; A7281; A7288; B1109; B1110; B1143; B1183; B1194; B1256; B1283; B1307; B8914; B8941; C775; C797; C867; C878; C937; C955; C4601; C4673; C4814; C4844; C4845; C4846; C4847; C4861; C4862; D7912; D7978; D7981; D8088; E2366; E2573; E2586; F5814; F6131; F6206.

No 12 Squadron: B8914; C1031; C1037; C9837; C9982; D7914; D8059; E2220; E2233; E2476; E2506; E2533; E2630; E2643; E2833; E9578; E9609; F4402; F4410; F4412; F4413; F4414; F4425; F4426; F4429; F4435; F4442; F4465; F4529; F4661; F4845; F4847; F4855; F4856; F4865; F4875; F4877; F4879; F4893; F4895; F4898; F4900; F4942; F5140; H1514; H1566; H1568; H1569; H1571; H1574; H1581; H1589; H1594; H1596; H1599; H1669.

No 13 Squadron: C1042; D7812; F4369; F4448; F4488; F4503; F4516; F4572; F4708; F4737; F4948; F4955; F4957; H1440; H1623; H1627; J6594; J6694; J6710; J6743; J6766; J6800; J7660; J8290.

No 14 Squadron: J6593; J6648; J7629.

No 16 Squadron: B1112; C968; C986; F4513; F4519; F4957.

No 20 Squadron: A7141; A7144; A7164; A7180; A7184; A7193; A7203; A7210; A7211; A7213; A7214; A7215; A7234; A7241; A7248; A7250; A7253; A7255; A7256; A7271; A7285; A7294; A7298; A7299; B817; B883; B1104; B1110; B1111; B1112; B1114; B1116; B1122; B1125; B1126; B1130; B1132; B1133; B1138; B1139; B1156; B1168; B1177; B1191; B1209; B1232; B1279; B1304; B1307; B1344; C808; C843; C850; C859; C892; C904; C938; C951; C957; C976; C980; C987; C989; C4604; C4605; C4606; C4615; C4616; C4617; C4672; C4718; C4749; C4764; C4804; C4810; C4818; C4826; C4836; D7851; D7864; D7897; D7915; D7919; D7939; D7951; D7993; D8035; D8036; D8039; D8086; D8090; D8092; E2154; E2155; E2158; E2181; E2213; E2238; E2246; E2247; E2249; E2250; E2252; E2253; E2258; E2297; E2337; E2338; E2339; E2340; E2370; E2403; E2407; E2419; E2420; E2423; E2429; E2452; E2467; E2470; E2471; E2493; E2512; E2536; E2561; E2562; E2566; E2568; E2588; E2603; E2605; F4304; F4330; F4396; F4414; F4421; F4446; F4463; F4544; F4562; F4602; F4643; F4658; F4665; F4693; F4700; F4720; F4766; F4839; F4881; F4905; F4908; F4914; F4915; F4916; F4929; F4947; F4953; F4958; F6116; F6195; F6121; F9616; H1428; H1438; H1508; H1601; J6588; J6594; J6621; J6638; J6643; J6645; J6647; J6650; J6654; J6656; J6663; J6700; J6730; J6741; J6752; J6774; J6783; J6792; J7644; J7677; J7682; J7684.

No 21 Squadron: C986; D8025.

No 22 Squadron: A7118; A7144; A7149; A7151; A7161; A7162; A7163; A7169; A7172; A7174; A7178; A7179; A7181; A7185; A7189; A7201; A7204; A7205; A7207; A7223; A7226; A7230; A7233; A7239; A7243; A7251; A7265; A7268; A7279; A7281; A7286; A7300; B1101; B1103; B1104; B1105; B1112; B1114; B1115; B1121; B1123; B1136; B1152; B1155; B1162; B1164; B1168; B1171; B1182; B1188; B1209; B1213; B1217; B1253; B1330; C770; C776; C795; C840; C842; C901; C929; C961; C978; C989; C1003; C1038; C1040; C1045; C4631; C4706; C4747; C4808; C4810; C4828; C4832; C4835; C4848; C4888; C4894; D2676; D7894; D7908; D7986; D8089; E2203; E2243; E2269; E2408; E2410; E2453; E2454; E2466; E2477; E2499; E2500; E2601; F5820; F5823; F5824; H1594; H7062.

No 24 Squadron: D7864; F4341; F4571; F4688; F4878; F5996; H1460; H1604; H1617; J6681; J8249; J8258; J8262; J8265; J8273; J8430.

No 28 Squadron: D8036; E2442; E2605; F4614; F4630; F4634; F4636; FR4640; F4707; F4752; F4870; F4931; H1499; H1508; H1509; H1512; H1514; H1520; H1521; H1537; H1541; H1548; H1554; J6641; J6588; J6626; J6630; J6638; J6646; J6656; J6761; J6762; J6779; J6780; J6782; J6795; J7677.

No 31 Squadron: D7807; D7813; D8097; D8034; E2257; E2297; E2450; E2501; F4315; F4320; F4390; F4463; F4485; F4494; F4495; F4542; F4555; F4594; F4643; F4658; F4664; F4683; F4689; F4707; F4758; F4814; F4839; F4915; F4942; F4951; F4958; H1428; H1457; H1461; H1497; H1510; H1686;

J6621; J6623; J6625; J6634; J6640; J6641; J6647; J6649; J6650; J6651; J6652; J6654; J6657; J6675; J6750; J6754; J6757; J6758; J6761; J6771; J6782; J6796; J7683.

No 33 Squadron: B1186; C4698; D8003.

No 34 Squadron ('Z' Flight): B1185; B1212; B1214; B1230; C913; C4674; C4700; C993; C4755; C4757; C4758.

No 35 Squadron: B1134; B8919; C4849; D7903. (NB: Not to be confused with 35(T) Squadron, Northolt, which also flew Bristol F2Bs.)

No 36 Squadron: C4896.

No 39 Squadron: A7249; A7265; B1184; B1186; B1157; B1252; B1260; B1261; B1262; B1264; B1330; B1331; C964; C4635; C4636; C4638; C4639; C4646; C4650; C4670; C4671; C4815; C4850; D8001.

No 48 Squadron: A3318; A3320; A3322; A3323; A3324; A3325; A3327; A3330; A3334; A3336; A3337; A3338; A3340; A3341; A3343; A3346; A6213; A7101; A7107; A7108; A7109; A7110; A7111; A7114; A7115; A7116; A7117; A7121; A7123; A7137; A7146; A7150; A7151; A5153; A7155; A7164; A76166; A7170; A7171; A7176; A7177; A7182; A7187; A7195; A7213; A7216; A7217; A7219; A7220; A7221; A7222; A7224; A7225; A7727; A7229; A7254; A7262; A7277; A7290; A7295; A7298; B1108; B1113; B1115; B1117; B1124; B1126; B1134; B1152; B1181; B1182; B1187; B1190; B1192; B1193; B1231; B1265; B1269; B1271; B1299; B1337; B1769; C786; C808; C814; C841; C846; C855; C871; C883; C886; C926; C933; C940; C943; C962; C4603; C4606; C4628; C4640; C4701; C4707; C4816; C4831; C4864; C4886; D2167; D2676; D6041; D7900; D7902; D7909; D7936; D7984; D8027; D8061; E2260; E2282; E2413; E2455; E2458; E2480; E2507; E2510; E2511; E2522; E2524; E2534; E2596; E2608; E2610; E2611; F4311; F4377; F4403; F4408; F4425; F4442; F4470; F4488; F4625; F4627; F4637; F4861; F4878; F5809; F5811; F5817; F5995; H1530; H1544; H1552.

No 59 Squadron: A7129; C9853; C9897; C9973; D2660; D2708; D2755; D7860; D8087; E1978; E1992; E2014; E2015; E2016; E2028; E2030; E2050; F5117; F5118; F5130; F5132; F9606.

No 62 Squadron: B1207; B1211; B1216; B1219; B1234; B1238; B1245; B1246; B1247; B1250; B1251; B1267; B1268; B1273; B1336; B1339; B1341; B1343; C769; C779; C788; C796; C874; C895; C919; C944; C953; C959; C1002; C4609; C4619; C4630; C4633; C4637; C4703; C4709; C4744; C4746; C4751; C4824; C4859; C4887; D7897; D7899; D7945; D7948; D8028; E2182; E2218; E2244; E2256; E2457; E2468; E2475; E2479; E2497; E2509; E2513; E2515; E2525; E2528; E2595; E2598; F5168; F5812; H7065.

No 67 Squadron (1 AFC): A7184; A7188; A7190; A7192; A7194; A7196; A7198; A7200; A7202; A7236; A7237; A7239; A7273; B1123; B1125; B1128; B1129; B1140; B1146; B1147; B1148; B1149; B1150; B1178; B1198; B1199; B1205; B1222; B1223; B1225; B1227; B1229; B1276; B1278; B1280; B1284; B1285; B1286; B1287; B1295; B1298; C4622; C4623; C4624; C4625; C4626; C4627; C4730; C4840.

No 69 Squadron (3 AFC): C917; C995; E2529.

No 70 Squadron: D8095; F4925; J6622.

No 88 Squadron: B1187; B1231; B1234; B1341; B7947; C774; C777; C778; C780; C782; C783; C785; C787; C821; C825; C852; C870; C879; C922; C952; C983; C1000; C4601; C4720; C4867; C4880; D7905; D7914; D7942; D8023; D8026; D8062; D8064; E2153; E2183; E2216; E2220; E2263; E2451; E2458; E2459; E2474; E2481; E2506; E2533; E2579; E2610; F4442; F5997.

No 105 Squadron: F4330; F4332; F4334; F4380; F4616; F4651; F4801.

No 106 Squadron: F4380; F4796; H1441.

No 111 Squadron: A7190; A7194; A7196; A7200; A7237; A7288; B1129; B1147; B1198; B1287; B1293; B1296; B1298; B1317; C4725; C4727; C4732; C4840; C4899; D7918; D7993; E2288; E2290; E2293.

No 114 Squadron: E2248; F4630; F4634; F4636; F4640; H1499; H1509; H1512; H1514; H1520; H1541.

No 139 Squadron: B1185; B1212; B1214; B1230; C913; C916; C990; C991; C992; C993; C994; C996; C997; C999; C4674; C4700; C4754; C4755; C4756; C4757; C4758; C4759; C4760; C4762; D7957; D7960; D7963; D7966; D7969; D7972; D7975; D7978; D7986; D8047; D8060; D8063; D8065; D8066; D8069; D8072; D8075; D8078; D8081; D8084; E2185; E2186; E2187; E2188; E2189; E2190; E2285; E2291; E2292.

No 141 Squadron: C819; C820; C823; C849; C851; C858; C863; C875; C880; C887; C923; C977; C981; C997; C4631; C4715; C4778; C4822; D2157; D2212; D2245; D2248; D2262; D2362; D2368; D2411; D2478; D2535; D2574; D2585; D2604; D7987; E2604; F4306.

No 208 Squadron: C4651; D7819; D7838; D7839; D8096; E2299; FR4582; F4583; FR4588; FR4589; F4791; F4950; H1454; H1455; H1456; H1463; H1490; H1501; H1623; H1649; H1670; H1673; H1678; H1682; JR6767; JR6785; JR6788; JR6789; J6794; J6798; J7640.

Cambridge UAS: C4740; F4542; F4548; J8434.

Oxford UAS: J6685; J8250; J8257.

No 1 FTS: D7816; F4651.

No 2 FTS: C1018; F4389; F4420; F4618; H1425; H1430; H1460.

No 4 FTS: H1677.

No 5 FTS: C799; J8282.

RAF College, Cranwell: C763; C768; D2703; D8083; E1971; F4502; F4511; F4747; F4762; F4884; H1438; H1439; H1598; H1642; H1689; J6677; J6689; J6743; J6748; J6760.

School of Army Co-operation, Winchester: C1037; D8092; E2533; F4295; F4518; F4542; F4579; F4622; F4651; F4813; F4836; H1395; H1432; H1599; H1603; J6682; J6726; J6754.

School of Army Co-operation, Old Sarum: C1014; D7847; F4646; F4952; H1562; H1668.

Dept of CAS Command Flight, Northolt: F4387; F4491; F4496; F4913; J6729.

No 27 Group, Bircham Newton: F4805; F4806.

No 186 Development Unit, Gosport: E2564; E2607.

NFF, Biggin Hill: F4745; J6600; J6714.

RAF Quetta (unit unspecified): C803; D7809; F4541; J6781 ('B); J6782 ('C').

RAF Ismailia (unit unspecified): E2287; E2294; E2295; F4623; F4651; F4731; F4910; F4926; H1669; H1679.

RAE, Farnborough: B1201; C4654; C4776; F4329; F4360; F4587; F4675; F4728; H1450; J8263.

A&AEE, Martlesham Heath:: A7183; B1181; B1200; B1201; B1204; B1206; C4654; D7968; E2306; E2400; F4587; F4631; F4819; F4864; H1436; H1559; J6586; J6753; J6800; J8251 (various trials/tests).

5. Operational F2B Units as at 11 November 1918

Sqn/Unit	*Base*	*OC*	*Remarks*
No 9 Sqn	Premont	Maj J. T. Rodwell	Disbanded 31/12/19
No 11 Sqn	Bethencourt	Maj R. W. Heath	Disbanded 31/12/19
No 12 Sqn	Estourmel	Maj T. Q. Back	Disbanded 22/7/22
No 20 Sqn	Iris Farm	Maj E. H. Johnston	To India, May 1919
No 22 Sqn	Aniche	Maj J. A. McKelvie	Disbanded 20/11/19
No 33 Sqn	Kirton-in-Lindsey	Capt G. M. Turnbull	Disbanded 13/6/19
No 35 Sqn	Flaumont	Maj D. F. Stevenson DSO, MC	Disbanded 26/6/19
No 36 Sqn	Usworth	Maj J. H. S. Tyssen	Disbanded 13/6/19
No 39 Sqn	Bavichove	Maj W. T. F. Holland	Disbanded 16/11/18
No 48 Sqn	Reckem	Maj K. R. Park MC	Renumbered No 5 Sqn 1/2/20
No 59 Sqn	Caudry	Maj C. J. Mackay	Disbanded 4/8/19
No 62 Sqn	Villers-lez-Cagnicourt	Maj F. W. Smith	Disbanded 3/7/19
No 75 Sqn	North Weald	Maj C. S. Ross	Disbanded 13/6/19
No 76 Sqn	Ripon	Maj A. C. Wilson	Disbanded 10/8/19
No 88 Sqn	Bersee	Maj R. Stuart-Wortley MC	Disbanded 10/8/19
No 111 Sqn	Kantara	Maj S. H. Long DSO, MC	Renumbered No 14 Sqn, 1/2/20
No 138 Sqn	Chingford	?	Disbanded 1/2/19
No 139 Sqn	Arcade	Maj H. H. Kitchener	Disbanded 7/3/19
No 141 Sqn	Biggin Hill	Maj B. E. Baker	Disbanded 1/2/20
No 1 Sqn AFC	Ramleh	Maj S. W. Addison	To Australia, March 1919
No 3 Sqn AFC*	Premont	Maj D. V. J. Blake	No 69 Sqn RFC retitled 19/1/18; disbanded Feb 1919
'L' Flight	Auberchicour	Capt B. Catchpole MC, DFC	
'M' Flight	Menin	Capt A. W. F. Glenny MC, DFC	
'N' Flight	Estourmel	Capt C. E. Barrington	
'O' Flight	Premont	Capt E. J. Jones, MC, DFC	
'P' Flight	Cysoing	Capt L. H. Jones, DFC	

*One Flight only: see 'O' Flight.

6. British Civil Register F2Bs

G-EASH	Ex-H1376; ADC demonstrator; withdrawn from use April 1921
G-EASU	Ex-H1639; sold overseas September 1920
G-EASV	Ex-H1638; sold overseas November 1920
G-EAWA	Ex-H951; sold as scrap
G-EAWZ	Ex-H1282; crashed September 1921
G-EAYQ	Ex-H1389; to Belgium 13/10/21
G-EBAK	Ex-H1291; to Belgium 29/12/21
G-EBAL	Ex-H1292; to Belgium 2/3/22
G-EBAM	Ex-H1240; to Belgium 25/2/22
G-EBAT	Ex-H1242; crashed 28/1/22 en route to Belgium
G-EBAU	Ex-H1244; to Belgium 15/2/22
G-EBBD	Ex-D7842; to Belgium 28/1/22
G-EBBO	Ex-H1258; to Belgium 11/3/22
G-EBCN	Pattern aircraft for Belgium registration cancelled 24/7/23
G-EBCU	Ex-E2058; to Belgium 6/5/22
G-EBCV	Ex-H1281; to Belgium 12/7/22
G-EBCW	Ex-H1245; to Belgium 18/7/22
G-EBDB	Ex-E5219; to Belgium 12/7/22
G-EBDN	Ex-H927; to Belgium 12/7/22
G-EBEE	Ex-H926; to Belgium 18/7/22
G-EBFD	Ex-E2354; sold to Serbia March 1923
G-EBIO	Ex-H1254; scrapped 1935
G-ABXA	Ex-J8258; Ex-No 24 Squadron RAF; converted to air fuel tanker; withdrawn November 1934
G-ABXV	Ex-F4711; wrecked 18/9/33
G-ABYD	Ex-J8446; scrapped after accident March 1933
G-ABYE	Ex-F4721; registration cancelled April 1938
G-ABYF	Ex-J8429; dismantled 1939; registration cancelled August 1945
G-ABYL	Ex-J8444; scrapped 1933
G-ABYT	Ex-J8434; CUAS; scrapped after accident 1936
G-ABZG	Ex-J8245; No 2 Squadron RAF; scrapped May 1938
G-ACAA	Ex-F4516; No 13 Squadron RAF; registration cancelled December 1946
G-ACAC	Ex-J8437; scrapped January 1936
G-ACCG	Ex-J6790; scrapped July 1939
G-ACFK	Ex-J8285; sold as scrap May 1936
G-ACFL	Ex-C4897; sold as scrap May 1936
G-ACFN	Ex-F4542; No 31 Squadron RAF; School of Army Co-operation, Winchester; CUAS; sold for scrap May 1936
G-ACFO	Ex-C4750; sold for scrap May 1936
G-ACFP	Ex-F4434; sold for scrap January 1938
G-ACHR	Ex-F4342; crashed in France 19/9/33
G-ACPE	Ex-J8448; scrapped January 1939
G-ADJR	Ex-J8455; scrapped January 1938
G-AEPH	Ex-D8096; registration reserved 1936; Shuttleworth Collection 1985
G-AFHJ	Ex-F4587; RAE; destroyed by enemy action World War 2

Derivatives

Though not strictly civilianised F2Bs per se, the following aircraft were direct 'descendants' of the basic F2B design:

G-EAIZ	Tourer, Type 29: registered 7/8/19; demonstration a/c: withdrawn September 1920
G-EANR	Tourer, Type 29: registered 23/9/19; sold USA May 1920
G-EART	Tourer, Type 47: Instone Air Line: withdrawn February 1921
G-EAUE	Seely, Type 36: one only built; converted to Type 85, serial J7004
G-EAVU	Tourer, Type 47: dual demo a/c for Spain; scrapped September 1921
G-EAWB	Tourer, Type 29: withdrawn 30/12/21
G-EAWQ	Tourer, Type 28: Spain (M-AAEA), crashed 23/4/21
G-EAWR	Tourer, Type 47: delivered Madrid 24/4/21 (M-AEAA)
G-EAXA	Tourer, Type 29: convert to Type 81 Puma; crashed 10/5/24
G-EAXK	Tourer, Type 28: to Australia (G-AUDF); crashed 27/1/25
G-EBFR	Type 81 Puma trainer: crashed June 1923
G-EBFS	Type 81 Puma trainer: scrapped May 1924
G-EBFT	Type 81 Puma trainer: crashed 10/3/25
G-EBFU	Type 81 Puma trainer: crashed 1928
G-EBGF	Type 76 Jupiter Fighter: crashed 23/11/23
G-EBHG	Type 76B Jupiter Fighter: to Sweden (Army 4300/1300/3667; civil SE-AEE); crashed 19/9/37
G-EBHH	Type 76A Jupiter Fighter: converted Type 89; wrecked in collision with G-EBJA 23/9/25
G-EBIH	Type 89: wrecked in air collision 20/8/29
G-EBJA	Type 89: wrecked in collision with G-EBHH 23/9/25
G-EBJB	Type 89: crashed/burned 15/12/25
G-EBJC	Type 89: not completed
G-EBML	Type 89: written off 14/5/27
G-EBMN	Type 89: written off 17/3/27
G-EBNZ	Type 89: withdrawn October 1929 and written off 14/1/30
G-EBOA	Type 89: crashed 15/3/27
G-EBOC	Type 89A: wrecked in collision with G-AAWJ 7/7/31

G-EBOD	Type 89A: crashed 26/5/27 and written off 14/1/30
G-EBQS	Type 89A: withdrawn June 1929; written off 14/1/30
G-EBQT	Type 89A: crashed 23/8/28
G-EBSB	Type 89A: written off 14/1/30
G-EBSH	Type 89A: withdrawn from use November 1933
G-EBVR	Type 89A: written off 14/1/30
G-EBWN	Type 89A: withdrawn July 1929
G-EBYL	Type 89A: withdrawn October 1933
G-AAGF	Type 89A: written off August 1935
G-AALO	Type 89A: written off August 1935
G-AAWJ	Type 89A: wrecked in collision with G-EBOC 7/7/31
G-ABPL	Type 89A: written off December 1934
G-ABPM	Type 89A: written off August 1935

NB: Additional civil derivatives supplied directly to overseas countries are mentioned in chapter 'Civil Sons'.

7. Technical Data

As with all types of manufactured aircraft, the figures given below are specific to one individual aircraft's test results, and should not be regarded as concrete for every other machine of the same type.

DIMENSIONS	**F2A RR Falcon I**	**F2B RR Falcon III**	**F2B Mk IV RR Falcon III**
Span:	39ft 3in	39ft 3in	39ft 3in
Length:	26ft 3in	26ft 2in	26ft 5in
Height:	9ft 6in	9ft 9in	9ft 7½in
Chord:	5ft 6in	5ft 6in	5ft 6in
Gap:	5ft 4½in	5ft 4½in	5ft 4½in
Stagger:	17.1in	16.9in*	18.1in:
Dihedral:	3.5°	3.5°	3° 30′
Wheel track:	5ft 5¼in	5ft 5¼in	5ft 5½in
Tail span:	12ft	12ft 10in	13ft 9½in

*A7177 and B1101 et seq 18.1in.

PERFORMANCE	**F2A RR Falcon I**	**F2B Mk I RR Falcon III**	**F2B Mk IV RR Falcon III**
Max speed:	110mph	123mph	125mph
Climb to 10,000ft:	14½min	11¼min	11½min
Service ceiling:	16,000ft	20,000ft	20,000ft
Endurance:	3¼hr	3hr	3hr

WEIGHTS	**F2A RR Falcon I**	**F2B Mk I RR Falcon III**	**F2B Mk IV RR Falcon III**
Empty:	1,727lb	1,934lb	2,200lb
Military load:	180lb	185lb	185lb
Crew:	360lb	360lb	360lb
Fuel/oil:	486lb	300lb	438lb
Loaded:	2,753lb	2,779lb	3,350lb

COSTS
Airframe (minus engine, instruments, guns): £1,350.19s.0d
Rolls-Royce Falcon (I, II and III): £1,210.0s.0d
Sunbeam Arab: £1,017.10s.0d

ENGINES EMPLOYED
120hp Beardmore: R2A
150hp Hispano-Suiza: R2B
190hp Rolls-Royce Falcon I: F2A
150hp Hispano-Suiza: F2A, A3304 only
190hp Rolls-Royce Falcon I: F2B
220hp Rolls-Royce Falcon II: F2B
275-280hp Rolls-Royce Falcon III: F2B
200hp Hispano-Suiza: F2B
200hp Sunbeam Arab: F2B
200hp RAF 4d: F2B
180hp Wolseley W4A Viper: F2B
230hp Siddeley Puma: F2B
290hp Siddeley Puma: F2B, high compression
300hp Hispano-Suiza: F2B
290hp Liberty 8: USA 0-1
400hp Liberty 12: USA 0-1
300hp Wright H: US XB-1A

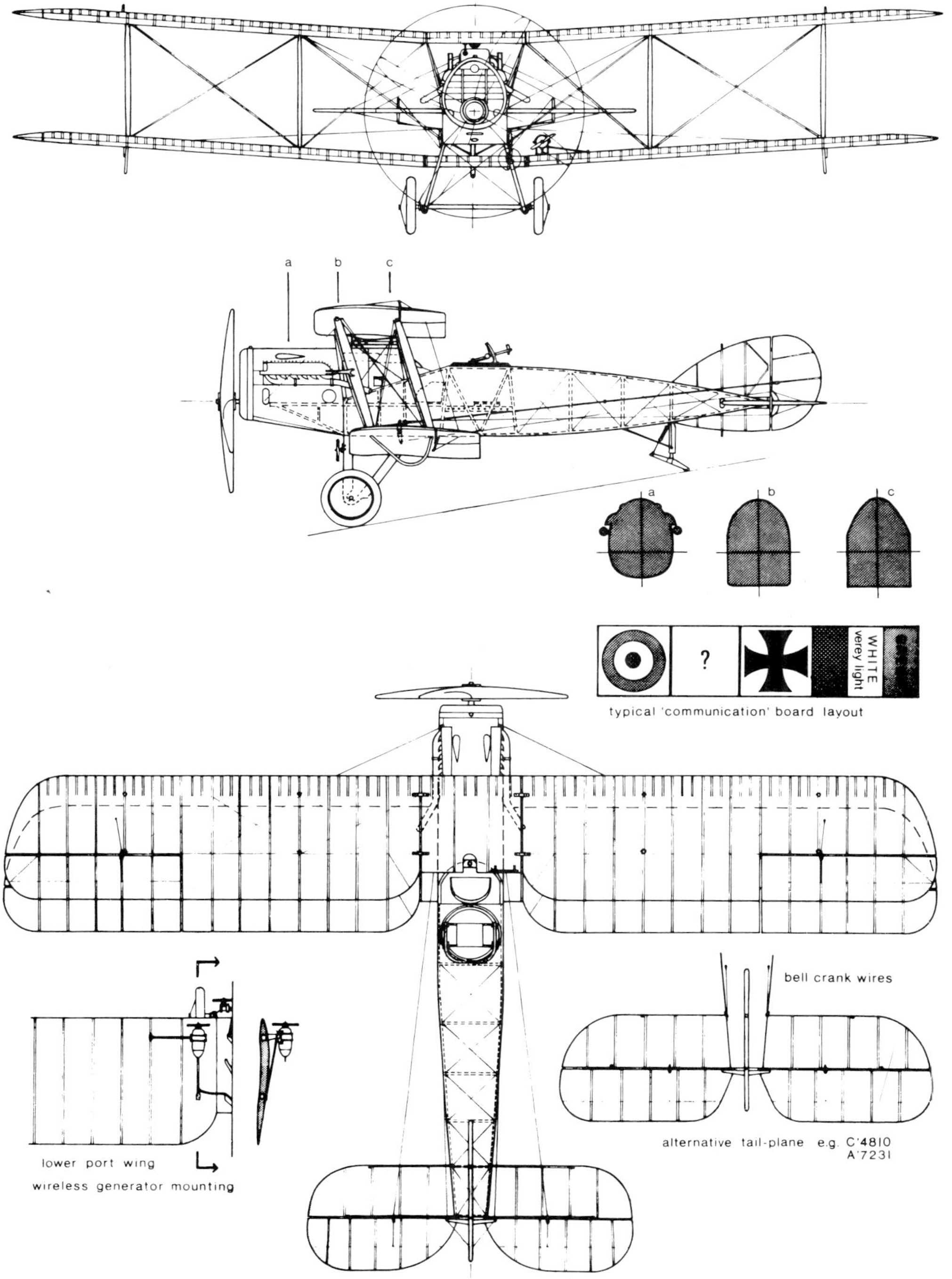

BRISTOL F.2B FIGHTER

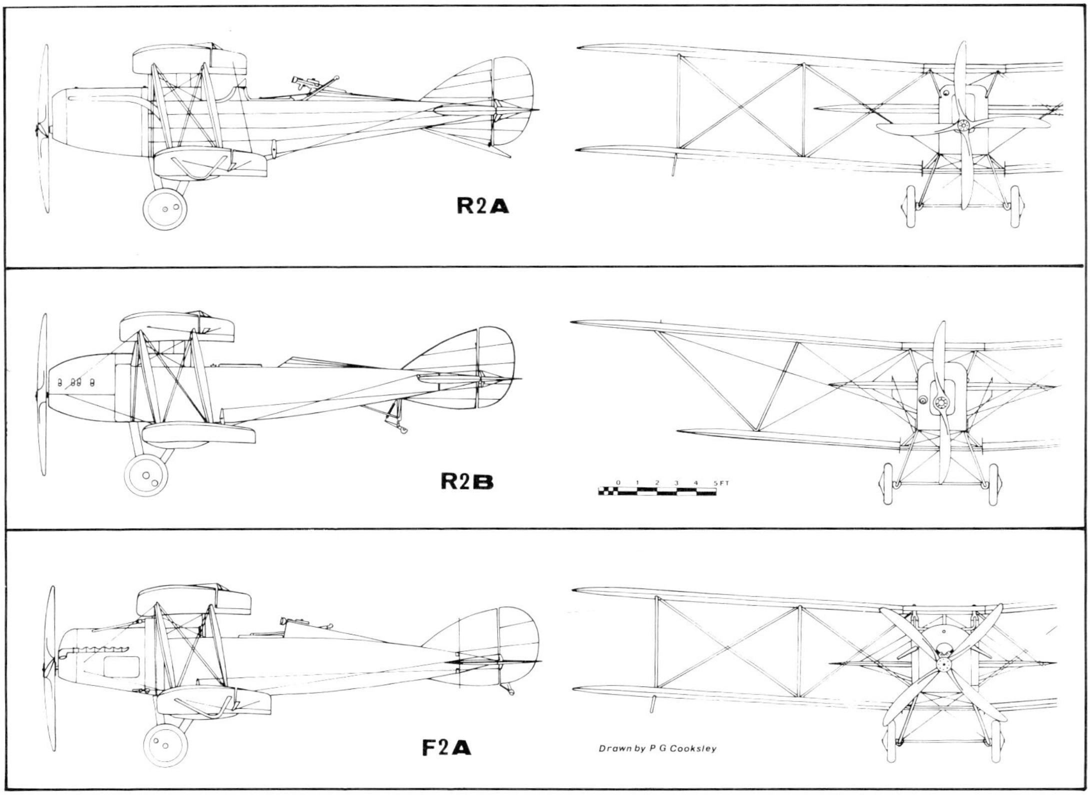

350hp Packard 1A-1327: US XB-1A, experimental
400hp Curtiss D-12: US XB-1A, experimental

ARMAMENT
F2A and F2B Mk 1
One fixed 0.303in Vickers machine gun with CC Gear forward. Single (or pair of) 0.303in Lewis machine guns on Scarff No 2 Ring, rear. Up to 12 25lb Cooper HE bombs under fuselage and wings.

F2B Mk IV
Forward gun, 0.303in Vickers Mk 1*, with CC Gear and 1.8in Aldis sight. Rear gun, Lewis 0.303in Mk III, on Scarff No 2 Ring, with Norman 100/100 Wind Vane Sight.

Total 750 rounds of 0.303in ammunition for forward gun. Six 97-round magazines for rear Lewis gun.

Provision for:
Four 25lb Cooper HE or two 112lb HE bombs, bottom centre and outer wings. Fitting for camera gun, bottom centre-plane, at port side. Installation of P.7 camera. Wireless and heating equipment. High Altitude Mk 1A bomb sight on starboard side of fuselage. Autoslots fitted, upper mainplanes. Equivalent ballast for absent gunner on carrier below rear cockpit.

8. F2A/F2B Bristol Type Numbers

In 1923 Frank Barnwell reviewed all Bristol-built or projected aircraft dating back to August 1914 and allotted to them retrospective Type numbers in strict chronological order. Thus, where in this volume's text a Type number is mentioned in the range Nos 1 to 89, it should be borne in mind that such Type numbers did not exist in the *contemporary* year(s) indicated. It follows therefore that, speaking historically, only the Bristol F2B Mk III and Mk IV could pedantically and correctly be termed Types 96 and 96A in their *contemporary* scene. The following listing gives every allotted Type number for every F2A, F2B, and their variants, and derivative designs.

Type No	*Name*	*Engine*	*Year*
12	F2A	190hp Rolls-Royce	1916
13	MR1	150hp Hispano Suiza	1916
14	F2B, Mks 1 and II	Rolls-Royce Falcon	1917
15	F2B	Sunbeam Arab	1917
16	F2B	200hp Hispano Suiza	1917
17	F2B	300hp Hispano Suiza	1918
17A	F2B (Frise ailerons)	300hp Hispano Suiza	1924
17B	F2B (enlarged tail)	300hp Hispano Suiza	1926
27	F2B Coupe	Rolls-Royce Falcon	1919
28	Tourer (three-seat Coupe)	Siddeley Puma	1919
29	Tourer (two-seat open)	Siddeley Puma	1919
34	Tourer seaplane (three-seat)	Viper	1919
36	Seely	Siddeley Puma	1919
40	F2B Mk 1 (late production)	Siddeley Puma	1919
41	Tourer seaplane (two-seat)	Beardmore	1919
47	Tourer (three-seat open)	Siddeley Puma	1920
48	Type 47 seaplane version	Siddeley Puma	1920
76	Jupiter Fighter	Jupiter	1923
76A	Jupiter Fighter G-EBHH	Jupiter	1923
76B	Swedish Fighter	Jupiter	1923
81	Convert Type 29 dual trainer	Siddeley Puma	1923
81A	Type 81, Greek version	Siddeley Puma	1925
85	Seely with RAE supercharger	Jupiter (S)	1923
86	Tourer two-seat	Rolls-Royce Falcon	1923
86A	Three-seat version of Type 86	Rolls-Royce Falcon	1923
88	Bulgarian Tourer, first version	Viper	1923
88A	Bulgarian Tourer, second version	Viper	1926
89	Advanced trainer (Type 81 conversion)	Jupiter	1924
89A	Type 89, ply fuselage	Jupiter	1926
96	F2B Mk III (revised)	Rolls-Royce Falcon	1925
96A	F2B Mk IV, Handley Page slotting	Rolls-Royce Falcon	1927

9. The Ballad of the Bristol Fighter

The following verses were composed by Harold Tetley Burt c1918 under the semi-pseudonym 'H.T.B.'. Burt died in 1923.

There are half-a-dozen 'buses
On which I've done a whack
From the RE8 to the three-ton weight
Of the lumbering old "Big-Ack"*
On a rotary-engined Avro
I've attempted several tricks
And I'm quite a dab at steering a "Crab"
(Better known as a DH6).

And many a first-class joyride
Have I had on them, last and first,
And many a strut have I had go phut
And many a wheel-tyre burst;
But none of them know the secret
Of making my heart rejoice
Like a well-rigged Bristol Fighter
With a Two-Six-Four Rolls-Royce.

She stands at her place on the tarmac
Like a tiger crouched for a spring
From the arching spine of her fuselage-line
To the ample spread of her wing,
With her wires like sinews tautened
And her tail-skid's jaunty twist
While her grey-cowled snout juts firmly out
Like a boxer's tight-clenched fist.

Is there a sweeter music
Or a more contented sound
Than the purring "clop" of her broad-curved prop
As it gently ticks around?
Then open her up crescendo
With a deep-toned swelling roar
Till she quivers and rocks as she strains
at the chocks
And clamours amain to soar.

Whisk them away me hearties!
Taxi her into the wind
Then off we skim on a spinning rim
With the tail well up behind.
Hold her down to a hundred
Then up in a climbing turn
Till we catch our breath in the air up high

I wouldn't exchange my seat, not I
For a thousand pounds to burn.
Air Force Songs & Verses; Aeronautics Ltd, 1927
*Armstrong Whitworth FK8

In contrast, perhaps, to Burt's unabashed eulogy is the following ditty composed by RAF crews on the North West Frontier of India in 1920; set to the music of the tune 'Old-Fashioned Mother of Mine'.

There's an old-fashioned Bristol
With old-fashioned planes
With a fabric all tattered and torn.
An old-fashioned engine that starts with a roar
And a sound like a thousand tin cans.
Tho' she won't loop or spin
'Cos she's nearly done in
Still there's something that makes her divine.
For she's quite safe and sound
'Cos she won't leave the ground
Will that old-fashioned Bristol of mine.

Select Bibliography

Bristol aircraft since 1910 — C. Barnes; Putnam, 1970
Aeroplanes of the RFC (Military Wing) — J. Bruce; Putnam, 1982
Fighters, Vol 1 — J. Bruce, Macdonald, 1965
The Bristol Fighter — J. Bruce; *Flight*, 7 November 1952
The Bristol Fighter — J. Bruce; *Profile* No 21
British Aeroplanes, 1914-18 — J. Bruce; Putnam, 1957
Air Board Technical Notes — Air Ministry, 1918
Air Publications AP 866, 2nd edition — Air Ministry, 1928
The War in the Air, Vols 3-6, Apps — H. A. Jones; OUP, 1931-37
Official history, Australia, 1914-18, Vol 8 — F. Cutlack; AWM, 1923
Australian Flying Corps, 1914-19 — C. Schaedel; Kookaburra, 1972
Aircraft of the RAF since 1918 — O. Thetford; Putnam, 1976
Curtiss aircraft, 1907-1947 — P. Bowers; Putnam, 1979
The British fighter since 1912 — P. Lewis; Putnam, 1967
British civil aircraft since 1919, Vol 1 — A. J. Jackson; Putnam, 1973
The Air Defence of Britain, 1914-18 — C. Cole/ F. Cheesman; Putnam, 1984
Fighter squadrons of the RAF — J. Rawlings; Macdonald, 1969
Coastal & Support squadrons of the RAF — J. Rawlings; Jane's, 1982
Bristol F2b Fighters, RAF 1918-32 — C. Bowyer; *Profile* No 237
Flying Minnows — 'Vee' (V Voss); J. Hamilton, 1935
Letters from a Flying Officer — R. S. Wortley; OUP, 1928
Hell in the Heavens — A. Whitehouse; W. & R. Chambers, 1938
The Clouds Remember — Bridgman/Stewart; Gale & Polden, 1936
Aces & Kings — L. Sutherland; J. Hamilton, 1936
The Central Blue — MRAF Sir J. Slessor; Cassell, 1956
Flying Years — C. H. Keith; J. Hamilton, 1937
Six Squadron — C. D. Stewart; RAF, 1963
IX Squadron — T. Mason; Beaumont, 1965
Leads the Field (12 Squadron) — T. Mason; Private, 1960
Pi in the Sky — W. Harvey; C. Huston, 1971
First in Indian skies — N. Franks; RAF Collection, 1982
AAHS Journal, Vol 17, No 2 — 1972
Cross & Cockade (GB) Journal — Various, 1970-84
Flying between the wars — A. Wheeler; Foulis, 1972
History of the Polish Air Force — J. B. Cynk; Osprey, 1972
Germany's Last Knight of the Air — P. Kilduff; Kimber, 1979